COURT MARTIAL CASES

COURT MARTIAL CASES

Defense Strategies and Best Practices

Attorneys Robert Capovilla,
Mickey Williams, Daniel Higgins,
Sean Flood, Josh Conklin and Brad Simon

Although the authors have made every reasonable effort to ensure that the information in this book is correct, the authors do not assume and hereby disclaims any liability to any party for any loss, damage, or disruption caused by errors or omissions, whether such errors or omissions result from negligence, accident, or any other cause.

Copyright © 2024 by Capovilla & Williams LLC

All rights reserved. No part of this book may be reproduced or transmitted in any form or by any means, electronic or mechanical, including photocopying, recording, or any information storage and retrieval system, without permission in writing from the authors.

ISBN: 978-1-6653-0704-8 - Paperback
eISBN: 978-1-6653-0705-5 - eBook

These ISBNs are the property of BookLogix for the express purpose of sales and distribution of this title. The content of this book is the property of the copyright holder only. BookLogix does not hold any ownership of the content of this book and is not liable in any way for the materials contained within. The views and opinions expressed in this book are the property of the Authors/Copyright holders, and do not necessarily reflect those of BookLogix.

Printed in the United States of America

Library of Congress Control Number: 2024914810

♾This paper meets the requirements of ANSI/NISO Z39.48 1992 (Permanence of Paper)

1 0 2 1 2 4

Contents

Introduction		vii
Get to Know the Authors		xi
Chapter 1	**Pre-Preferral of Charges**	1
Chapter 2	**Preferral of Charges**	21
Chapter 3	**The Article 32 Preliminary Hearing**	27
Chapter 4	**Referral of Charges and Convening the Court**	35
Chapter 5	**Initial Appearance and Arraignment**	43
Chapter 6	**Your Right to Discovery**	49
Chapter 7	**The Motions Hearing**	59
Chapter 8	**Military Rule of Evidence 412: The Rape Shield Law**	65

| Chapter 9 | Military Rule of Evidence 413: The "He Has Done It Before" Rule | 71 |

The Trial Process

Chapter 10	**Panel Selection**	79
Chapter 11	**Opening Statements: Tell Your Story**	85
Chapter 12	**Direct Examination: In Another's Eyes**	93
Chapter 13	**Cross-Examination: Win Your Story**	101
Chapter 14	**Closing Argument**	131
	Conclusion	143

Introduction

If you're a U.S. service member accused of a crime, you probably already know there's a long and winding legal road ahead. As if the accusation weren't stressful enough on its own, trying to stay on top of the process as charges are filed, court-martial hearings are scheduled, and the trial unfolds can be overwhelming, and the stakes seem to get higher as you round every corner. *Court Martial Cases: Defense Strategies and Best Practices* by attorneys Robert F. Capovilla and Mickey Williams, walks you through your legal journey from start to finish, explaining the procedures taking place at each stage and offering advice and examples drawn from their own experience defending members of the armed forces. A book can't take away all of the stress you're under at this time, but it can alleviate the uncertainty and anxiety that comes with not knowing what to expect on the road ahead.

This book isn't a novel you have to read from start to finish—it's a *guide*. No matter where you are in the legal process, you can go directly to the chapter that speaks to your current situation.

Introduction

There you'll find the information you need to make good decisions for your case. There are 14 chapters in total, each with a title clearly identifying the stage in the process it deals with. Each chapter is also preceded by a concise summary of its main points and ends with a quick overview of its takeaways. This enables you to see at a glance if a specific chapter covers the topics you need in the moment, or will need in the weeks or months ahead. For the most part, the *Guide* focuses on the process of putting together a solid defense in sexual assault cases, but the stages of the legal journey outlined here apply to other kinds of criminal charges as well. Having the knowledge and perspective provided by the *Guide* will help you work productively with your attorney as you prepare to defend your case.

The 14 chapters in this book walk you through every stage of a military criminal offense charge. Chapter 1 covers the uncertain and often confusing period between being accused and the filing, or preferral, of charges. This is the investigative phase of the process, when law enforcement begins to collect the evidence it needs to charge you with the commission of a crime. This is the time to hire an attorney: you need a team conducting its own investigation at this stage, and you don't want to do it yourself since your personal involvement could be construed as obstruction of justice. Later in the process you'll be assigned a military defense lawyer (this is covered in Chapter 4), but you're free to hire a civilian attorney to represent you at any point. The period before the preferral of charges is a smart time to do that.

Chapters 2 through 9 tell you how charges are preferred and the court-martial convened, what to expect from preliminary hearings, how the discovery phase of a trial works, and the role special rules dealing with sexual assault charges might play in your case. In Chapter 3, you'll learn about the Article 32 hearing, where the prosecutor and a hearing officer determine whether there is probable cause to charge you with the crime you stand accused of. The process by which the judge, prosecutor, and military defense counsel are selected and assigned to your court-martial are outlined in Chapter 4. Your first appearance before the court-martial judge is covered in Chapter 5, which deals with the arraignment hearing. This hearing launches the discovery phase of the trial, covered in Chapter 6. A second pre-trial hearing, called a motions hearing, in which the attorneys from both sides hash out the rules for the introduction of evidence during the trial itself, is discussed in Chapter 7. Chapters 8 and 9 examine two rules specific to sexual assault cases that might be factors in the decision about admissible evidence worked out in the motions hearing.

The remaining chapters of the *Guide* cover the trial itself, from panel selection to closing arguments. (What civilian trials refer to as a jury is called a panel in courts-martial.) Chapter 10 describes the question-and-answer method known as *voir dire* that attorneys use to select a fair and open-minded panel. As your attorney's first interaction with the panel, voir dire is crucial to establishing credibility and rapport. Arguments in the trial begin with opening statements, your defense team's first chance to tell your story and allow the panel to see the events in question from your point of view. Opening statements are covered in Chapter 11. Your story is told again throughout the trial, in the testimony of witnesses elicited during direct and cross examination. These two very different approaches to witness examination are described in Chapters 12 and 13. When everyone has had their say, and all of the evidence has been presented, your attorney tells your story one last time in the closing argument, outlined in Chapter 14.

If you're not picking up this book until the night before your arraignment, start at Chapter 5. If you don't find your way to this resource until your attorney is at work selecting the panelists for your trial, start at Chapter 10. Use this book in whatever way helps you get a handle on what is happening, what's at stake, and what comes next. Robert Capovilla and Mickey Williams have the experience and deep knowledge of military law and procedures to guide you through this complex, often stressful process. With thousands of military defense cases under their belts, the partners at Capovilla & Williams know the ins and outs of criminal trials in the military and what it takes to win them.

Get to Know the Authors

Robert F. Capovilla

Robert is a founding member of Capovilla & Williams, a law firm dedicated to defending the rights of service members nationwide, and a former military prosecutor and defense attorney in the Army JAG Corps. Military officials and clients alike see him as one of the most talented and charismatic trial attorneys in the field: "the best trial lawyer I have seen in my 18 years as a military attorney," says one senior official; "an absolute natural in the courtroom" and "an exceptional advocate who is cool and calm under pressure," others attest. As one of the most successful military sexual assault defense attorneys in the country, Robert has worked on thousands of sexual assault cases all over the United States, on six different continents, and across each of the five branches of the Armed Forces.

In 2019 Robert was selected as a Premier Lawyer of America and named a Top 40 trial attorney in the United States for attorneys under 40.

Recently, the National Trial Lawyers Association nominated him as a Top 40 trial attorney in the nation in criminal law, a distinction granted only the most qualified attorneys from each state or region. He has served as a guest lecturer in military justice at Georgia State Law School, where he taught students about the courts-martial process, and he was asked to speak to the Georgia Bar Association, where he lectured on military law, discharge upgrades, and separation boards. He has also taught classes on military rules of evidence, cross-examination, and the importance of a great opening statement. Most recently, he was asked to present to the Georgia National Guard Legal Command, where he answered questions for high-ranking legal officers and military judges on cross-examination, case theme and theory, and the importance of winning the jury's trust.

Before entering private practice, Robert was an active-duty judge advocate in the Army JAG Corps. While serving as a Judge Advocate, he was hand-selected by JAG Corps leadership to work on some of the most complex, difficult cases in the Corps. As a defense attorney, he worked on high-profile cases covered by major news outlets such as CNN, ABC News, and Fox News. In addition to serving as an attorney for the Trial Defense Services, he gained valuable litigation experience as both a trial counsel and a special assistant United States Attorney. Having worked as a military prosecutor and defense counsel, he possesses the experience, judgment, and skill to ensure that your rights will be protected throughout each and every step of the military justice process.

In private practice, Robert focuses much of his time on representing service members who have been accused of sexual assault. He has earned acquittal after acquittal on sexual assault cases at military posts all over the world, and has won several two-victim sexual assault cases, alcohol-related sexual assault cases, and husband-wife sexual assault cases. He prides himself on investigating every facet of a sexual assault case to discover the truth, and he's truly passionate about defending service members who have been falsely accused of sexual assault. In today's political climate, Robert Capovilla will even the playing field.

Mickey Williams

Mickey is also a founding member of Capovilla & Williams. As an Army Ranger, Mickey knows how to fight for what he believes in. The same discipline, work ethic, and tenacity that drove him as a war fighter are what drive him in the courtroom today as a passionate and devoted military justice defense attorney. As a trial attorney, Mickey has been described as a "rock star with an uncanny ability to relate to his audience with vivid and convincing storytelling." After a recent case, a veteran military judge said that Mickey's closing argument was "the best I've ever seen, and I've been doing this a long time." In describing Mickey's trial skills, a colleague simply stated: "You can't teach what he can do."

Immediately after graduating high school in 2002, Mickey joined the Army as an 11B Infantryman under a Ranger Regiment contract. After surviving the rigors of basic training in Fort Benning, GA, he went to Airborne school, jumped out of perfectly good airplanes, and trained for his biggest test at that time: the Ranger Indoctrination Program (RIP), now known as the Ranger Assessment and Selection Phase (RASP). Out of 200 initial RIP candidates, only 34 remained on graduation day: Mickey was one of them.

Shortly after graduation, he was assigned to B Company, 1st Ranger Battalion, 75th Ranger Regiment. While at the Ranger Regiment, Mickey went on four combat deployments to Iraq and Afghanistan. He participated in over 100 combat missions, including the initial invasion of Iraq, the rescue of POW Jessica Lynch, and the capture of dozens of terrorists. He also knew and served with CPL Pat Tillman, the former NFL legend who sacrificed his life for his country while at the 75th Ranger Regiment. Along the way, Mickey earned his Ranger Tab, Combat Infantry Badge, Air Assault Badge, and Expert Infantry Badge. He has operated closely with SOCOM forces such as the Navy SEALs, Green Berets, Air Force Pararescue (PJ), and Delta Force.

In 2006, Mickey ended his enlisted career and attended the University of Oregon, where he earned his bachelor's degree. From there, he went on to the Willamette University College of Law, where he excelled. In 2013, Mickey became a member of the Oregon State Bar and was commissioned into the United States Army Judge Advocates General (JAG) Corps. He was assigned to Fort Lee, Virginia, where he was selected to practice in military justice as a prosecutor.

The military judge also appointed Mickey a part-time military magistrate. As a military magistrate, Mickey presided over pre-trial confinement hearings and issued warrants for seizing or searching for evidence. He was also tasked with analyzing whether law enforcement could arrest soldiers for alleged misconduct. Mickey served as an Article 32 investigating officer and legal advisor for 15-6, and a financial liability and property loss investigator. He regularly provided legal advice to a Brigade Commander and Brigadier General.

After three years as a military prosecutor, Mickey requested a transfer to be a military defense attorney. His request was granted, and he was sent to the busiest legal jurisdiction in the United States Army: Fort Campbell, KY. He practiced there as a defense attorney and achieved stunning results for cases that included charges for murder, sexual assault, assault and battery cases, domestic violence, and all cases covering the spectrum of charges under the Uniform Code of Military Justice (UCMJ).

Why We Do What We Do

Robert and Mickey enjoyed successful careers in the armed forces, and served with passion and pride. Neither believed he would ever leave. As JAG officers who at various times worked as judges, prosecutors, and defense attorneys, they participated in the full scope of the military justice process. They learned its rules, its culture, the pressures it operates under, its priorities, and even its biases and limitations in ways only true insiders can.

One of these limitations, they recognized, was the ability of JAG-appointed defense counsels to freely and fully defend clients from within a chain of command that was subject to broader political influences and pressures. The defense of service members accused of sexual assault, in particular, was sometimes constrained by social and political concerns, placing personnel accused of these crimes at a disadvantage. When they began working for JAG's Trial Defense Services, Robert and Mickey realized they couldn't truly serve their clients from within the chain of command and separated from the U.S. Army.

Walking away from military careers they were so invested in—careers that offered security, a clear and predictable professional path, and a comfortable perch for themselves and their families—was a risk. It took courage. Robert and Mickey found the courage they needed for this step in their commitment to service. For both, leaving the Army and setting up as civilian defense attorneys was the best way to protect the interests of America's servicemen and servicewomen in their most difficult hour.

Capovilla & Williams was founded in the belief that the accused's right to the best possible defense, guaranteed by the U.S. Constitution's sixth amendment, is a bedrock of American democracy and a bulwark against tyranny. All persons accused of a crime are entitled to a lawyer who will advocate on their behalf, fighting for due process and a fair hearing. Robert and Mickey created Capovilla & Williams so they could be a voice for the accused, without interference or pressure from anyone or anything but their own desire to protect and defend America's service members and uphold the Constitution.

Robert and Mickey have defended service members accused of sexual assault, sodomy, desertion, desertion during wartime, insubordination, obstruction of justice, solicitation, AWOL, fraternization, inappropriate relationship, larceny, drug possession, drug use, drug distribution, adultery, premediated murder, manslaughter, DUI, damage to government property, negligent homicide, attempted murder, attempted sexual assault, abusive sexual contact, fraud, conduct unbecoming, drunk and disorderly conduct, and fraternization, among others. They have been the voice of each and every marine, soldier, airman, and sailor they've defended, working with total commitment to ensure fair treatment and a just outcome for all of them.

Pre-Preferral of Charges

Chapter 1

The time between being accused of a crime and the filing of charges against you is the investigative phase in a criminal case. During this period, your attorney will collect evidence in your defense, while law enforcement gathers evidence against you and your chain of command starts outlining charges and initiates proceedings. You may be placed in confinement during the pre-preferral period.

Many service members who are accused of a crime do not want to hire an attorney until they are officially charged. Typically, these clients will call me up, ask me about the court-martial process, tell me that the accuser is lying and say that the Army Criminal Investigation Division, (CID), the Naval Criminal Investigative Service (NCIS), or the Air Force Office of Special Investigations (OSI) wants to question them. They usually add that they are not ready to hire a military defense attorney.

These service members cannot imagine, for the time being, that their command will actually want to move forward with the case. They say things like, "but it's my word against hers," "everyone knows I would never sexually assault anyone," or "there's no evidence because I didn't rape anyone."

My advice to these individuals, if they are in fact being investigated for sexual assault, is always the same: Hire an experienced military defense attorney now. It can mean the difference between winning and losing your case.

In this chapter, I want to discuss what the pre-preferral or pre-charged phase of the case is, what steps the command must take when they find out someone has accused you of sexual assault, what steps law enforcement must take, what you and your accuser can expect to see happen, and what you can do to properly plan your defense to ensure that you do not fall victim to an incomplete or biased investigation. Even at this stage, the stakes are high. Tread carefully—and seek legal help.

What Does Pre-Preferral Mean?

The pre-preferral stage of a sexual assault case means that you are under investigation by a military law enforcement agency, a civilian law enforcement agency, or, sometimes, both at the same time for the same accusation.

Here's how it starts: Someone makes an allegation against you of sexual assault. Typically, this happens when the accuser tells a friend, loved one, or supervisor, or contacts a local victim advocate. The reality is that any person may report an offense, and any military authority may receive a report of offense.[1]

Ideally, if a service member receives a report of sexual assault, that service member should promptly inform their immediate commander.[2] However, it is not uncommon for reports of sexual assault to be made to law enforcement officials first. In this case, the law enforcement agency will contact the chain of command and inform them that an accusation has been made against you.

---

[1] R.C.M. 301- Report of Offense. Manual for Courts-Martial. 2019 Edition.
[2] I.D.

You are now officially under investigation. Your accuser has filed a report against you, and your command is aware that you have been accused. Law enforcement is now ready to start its investigation into the alleged misconduct.

If this is happening to you, don't speak to anyone other than an attorney about your case. Do not talk to law enforcement. Do not waive your rights. Do not think you can handle the situation on your own. You are wrong. Call the local Area Defense or Trial Defense office. Call an attorney.

What Your Chain of Command Can Do

Now that law enforcement is aware that you have been accused of sexual assault, your command has no choice but to take action. Commanders will not call off the dogs or tell law enforcement that you are simply not the kind of soldier, sailor, or airman to sexually assault anyone. They are going to do their jobs, even if you're the best supply NCO of all time.

It is important to recognize that each commander in your chain of command has independent yet overlapping discretion to handle ("dispose of") offenses within the limits of that commander's authority.[3] This means that if you are accused of disrespecting a commissioned officer, your company level commander can dispose of that offense as long as his superior commander does not have a withholding policy. This authority to dispose of an offense is called "initial disposition authority." It is important to note that sexual assault does not fall under this rule. Only commanders who possess special court-martial convening authority and are in the grade of 0-6 or higher have initial disposition authority for sexual assault cases.[4] More simply, the first 0-6 in your chain of command typically has initial disposition authority over the accusation made against you.

Each branch handles sexual assault allegations a little bit dif-

---

[3] R.C.M. 201- Report of Offense. Manual for Courts-Martial. 2019 Edition.
[4] See DoD Instruction 6495.02. "Sexual Assault Prevention and Response (SAPR) Program Procedures. March 28, 2013.

ferently. My goal here is not to precisely define how each branch functions at this stage of the investigation. Instead, I will give you a general breakdown of how the Army processes flags, as I have found that the Army's process is consistent with the other branches. This should provide you guidance whether you are a soldier, airman, sailor, marine, or coast guardsman.

Once the report of sexual assault is made, your commander will typically call you into her office. She will inform you that an allegation has been made, that you are under investigation, and that you must be "flagged." The "flag" process in the Army is governed by Army Regulation 600-8-2. According to this regulation, a flag is an abbreviated term used to describe the initiation or the removal of a suspension of favorable action.[5]

Here is the good news: just because you are flagged does not mean that your chain of command is going to court-martial you, and it does not mean that they think you are guilty. It is mandatory for commanders to initiate a flag for any soldier under investigation for sexual assault.[6] This is true even if the evidence against you is weak.

Here is the bad news: once you are flagged, you cannot be promoted, receive awards and decorations, re-enlist, attend military schools, or retire.[7] While this may seem unfair, it is a necessary precaution. Imagine what Congress would think if the Marine Corps allowed an E-8 to retire while under investigation for sexual assault. It would not look good.

Once you've been flagged, your career will essentially be at a standstill, and there is not a whole lot you can do about it. This is a good time to call an attorney if you have not done so already. Remain calm, maintain your military bearing, and understand that this is likely the beginning of a very long road. One point of emphasis: <u>do not talk to your commander about what happened</u>. Even if you tell her that you are entirely innocent, it will not matter. You are getting flagged.

---

[5] I.D.
[6] I.D.
[7] I.D.

What happens next? The Manual for Courts Martial (MCM) gives commanders several options to ensure that good order and discipline are upheld in their units. Here is a brief description of the steps your commander MAY take once you are accused of sexual assault:

1. Apprehension: Your command may take you into custody.[8] An apprehension is an arrest. This does not happen much in sexual assault cases. The rules are quick to point out that apprehension is different from being detained by law enforcement officials for investigation purposes, which may also happen.[9] Essentially, apprehension means that your command believes there is probable cause to suggest that you are guilty of sexual assault, and they hold you until actions are taken under the Rules for Courts-Martial sections 304 and 305. This form of restraint normally lasts only a short period and acts as a holdover device if command intends to place you into pretrial confinement. Again, in a strict sense, apprehension at this stage is relatively unusual in a sexual assault case.
2. Pretrial Restraint: Your command may place you under some form of pretrial restraint.[10] While apprehension is relatively unusual, pretrial restraint is very common. Pretrial restraint may consist of conditions on liberty, restriction in lieu of arrest, arrest, or confinement. For purposes of simplicity, I am going to focus on conditions on liberty because they are by far the most common acts of pretrial restraint a commander can take. Conditions on liberty include orders to report periodically to a specified

---

[8] R.C.M. 302 – Apprehension.
[9] I.D.
[10] R.C.M. 304- Pretrial Restraint

official, orders to not go to certain places, and orders to not associate with a certain person.

If you are accused of sexual assault, you will very likely be issued a no-contact order. The command is not going to let you go near the person who accused you of sexual assault. This is more typical if that person is also a service member, but it occurs in cases where the accuser was a civilian as well. Here is my best advice: follow the order.

You will be in violation of Article 92 of the Uniform Code of Military Justice (UCMJ) if you violate a lawfully imposed no-contact order. Do not do it. Do not contact your accuser, call your accuser, or text your accuser, and do not tell one of your friends to do any of those things. Just stay away. I have seen too many cases when my client won the sexual assault charge but lost the Article 92 charge simply because they tried to fix things themselves. Follow the order.

There is always a chance that the order is not lawful. Bring your no-contact order to your attorney. They will help you figure out what to do. Do not try to fix this yourself. You will only make it worse. Make sure you keep track of any form of pretrial restraint placed upon you, the documentation, and the conditions. Also, keep a diary of what the imposition authority tells you. This can all be helpful to your attorney down the road.

3. Pretrial Confinement: Your commander may place you in pretrial confinement.[11] This is a big deal. Your command has the power, under certain circumstances, to place you in jail until the date of your trial.

---

[11] R.C.M. 305 – Pretrial Confinement

Here is what you need to know:

A. Probable Cause – No person may be ordered into pretrial confinement unless probable cause exists.[12] Probable cause means there is a reasonable belief that you committed the offense of sexual assault, and confinement is required under the circumstances.[13]
B. Right to an Attorney – Request an attorney: you have the right to one.[14] Once a competent authority places you in pretrial confinement, your right to counsel is created. If requested by you, you must be provided counsel before the initial review or within 72 hours of your request, whichever occurs first.[15]
C. Action by the Commander – No later than 72 hours after you are placed in pretrial confinement, your commander must decide whether such confinement is necessary. In order to keep you in confinement, your commander must decide that you committed an offense triable by court-martial and that confinement is necessary because it is foreseeable that you will either not appear at trial or that you will engage in serious criminal misconduct, and that less severe forms of restraint are not adequate under the circumstances.
D. Entitled to a Hearing – Within seven days of being placed into pretrial confinement, you are

---

[12] R.C.M. 305(d)
[13] I.D.
[14] R.C.M. 305(f).
[15] I.D.

entitled to a hearing to challenge your confinement.[16] You and your counsel may submit evidence to help your case. Your commander will be represented by legal counsel, typically the prosecutor who is assigned to the case. The commander's representative must prove by a preponderance of the evidence that your confinement is necessary.[17] Once the hearing is over, the reviewing officer must approve your continued confinement or order your immediate release.[18]

E. The Confinement Facility – Not all military installations have confinement facilities. If your installation has an adequate confinement facility, you will be held in that facility. If your installation does not have an adequate confinement facility, you will be held at a local, county, or state facility. The installation will have an agreement with that local facility to house active duty service members. Make sure your attorney has a copy of that agreement. Oftentimes, local facilities outside of the installation will not be able to follow the requirements necessary to ensure that you are not subjected to pretrial punishment. If this is the case, and in the event you are convicted, the judge may grant you two- or three-days credit for every day you were subjected to unduly harsh conditions or pretrial punishment.[19]

Your attorney needs to be in constant contact with you when you are subjected to pretrial confinement. You need to make sure

---

[16] R.C.M. 305(i)(2)(A)(i).
[17] R.C.M. 305(i)(2)(A)(iii).
[18] R.C.M. 305(1)(2)(c).
[19] R.C.M. 305(k).

that you are keeping a daily journal of the activity happening in confinement. This will help your attorney ensure that your rights are being upheld.

If, after the hearing, you are ordered to remain in pretrial confinement, talk to your attorney about requesting that your commander release you from confinement. Any commander in your chain of command may release you from confinement at any time.[20] If that does not work, after referral, your attorney may petition the military judge to release you from pretrial confinement.[21] Here's my best advice: listen to your attorney. A good attorney will be honest with you about your chances of getting out of pretrial confinement. A good attorney may even tell you that pretrial confinement is in your best interest. This can be the case if you cannot stay out of trouble. I have personally had to give this advice to my clients on more than one occasion.

It is unusual for your command to place you in pretrial confinement based solely on an allegation of sexual assault. Typically, your command will allow you to continue some form of service. Over the years, the only times my clients have found themselves in pretrial confinement in a sexual assault case is because the client committed more misconduct, such as obstruction of justice, or there were additional charges on the charge sheet like absent without leave (AWOL). So, while your commander may try to put you in pretrial confinement based on a sexual assault allegation alone, that would be very rare.

If you are placed on restriction in lieu of arrest, arrested, or ordered into pretrial confinement, your attorney should be requesting that your case be expedited. RCM 704(a) requires that you be brought to trial within 120 days of preferral of charges or imposition of restraint. In other words, if you are in pretrial confinement or subjected to other significant restraints, the command needs to ensure that your case is a priority, and your attorney needs to hold their feet to the fire by submitting speedy

---

[20] R.C.M. 305(g).
[21] I.D.

trial requests. The system requires that your case be given priority for as long as you are subjected to the conditions listed above.

The Role of Law Enforcement

Each military investigation agency has its own regulations and training. This section of the book will not cover those regulations, but will be from a practical standpoint, focusing on my personal experience dealing with these agencies. I will address what they do, how they do it, and what you and your attorney need to know about these agencies.

Let me say this now: I have a tremendous amount of respect for law enforcement personnel. I have personally witnessed and encountered several law enforcement officers that want nothing more than the truth to prevail. Most of these officers are simply trying to do the very best job that they can. That being said, I have also encountered a number of very stubborn and blatantly biased investigators over the years. Few things make my blood boil more than a law enforcement officer with an agenda. I believe these types of officers are in the minority, but they are out there. Your attorney must be ready to deal with these misguided investigators during the investigation or on that fateful day when that officer takes the stand to testify against you in trial.

The Investigation

Once a sexual assault complaint is reported to law enforcement, they will commence their investigation. This section focuses primarily on how military law enforcement organizations such as the Army Criminal Investigation Division (CID), the Naval Criminal Investigative Service (NCIS), or the Air Force Office of Special Investigations (OSI) handle their investigations. If you are under investigation from a local civilian entity, this section should provide basic guidance, but each law enforcement unit is unique; therefore, not all the practices discussed in this book are universal.

Typically, the first thing that a military law enforcement agency will do is conduct a-recorded video interview with your accuser. This discussion will occur at a law enforcement facility where they have recording capabilities. Each law enforcement agency is strongly encouraged to record all interviews with your accuser. This does not always happen. Make sure that your attorney knows exactly where, when, and how many times your accuser was interviewed. This can be very important during the discovery phase of your trial.

When law enforcement interviews your accuser, they are typically trained to be as accommodating, friendly, and sensitive as possible. They are not trained to confront your accuser on inconsistencies or areas of her story that do not make sense. This means you should never rely on law enforcement to point out the weaknesses in your accuser's story because they will not do that. Ever. The most you might get is a note in the narrative portion of the Report of Investigation that simply states something like, "A.R.'s account is not corroborated by the eyewitness who observed A.R. dancing with the suspect." It is your attorney's job to identify those inconsistencies, investigate them, and ultimately expose them during cross-examination.

Accuser interviews can be as short as 15 to 20 minutes or as long as seven or eight hours. In the room with your accuser may be a special victim's counsel (SVC). This is your accuser's attorney. The SVC is in a confidential relationship with your accuser. Just like your attorney cannot disclose confidential communications without your permission, the SVC cannot disclose his client's confidential communications. It is not uncommon for the accuser to also have a close personal friend with her during the interview for support. If you know that a close personal friend was with your accuser during the interview, your attorney MUST interview that personal friend. If your accuser spoke to her SVC in the presence of her friend, those communications are no longer confidential and may be subject to discovery.

Once the victim interview is done, law enforcement will then work to corroborate or investigate your accuser's account of what occurred. Typically, during a victim interview, law enforcement will ask your accuser if there are any witnesses, if she spoke to anyone about the sexual assault, if she still has the clothes she was wearing, and if she texted anyone about the assault. Also, when the report is timely, law enforcement will ask your accuser if she will consent to a sexual assault forensic examination (SAFE).

The purpose of a SAFE is to preserve physical evidence of the alleged sexual assault that can be helpful to law enforcement in building a case.[22] The SAFE is conducted by a Sexual Assault Nurse Examiner (SANE).[23] The exam is designed to collect physical and forensic evidence, such as DNA. SAFE exams are tremendously personal, requiring your accuser to undress so that trace evidence may be collected from the clothing worn during the encounter. Oral evidence is typically collected, done by swabbing your accuser's saliva.[24] Hair (head and pubic) samples are also taken, and usually, a special lamp is used during the exam to identify the presence of fluids on your accuser's body.[25]

From a general standpoint, SANEs are trained to collect and preserve as much evidence from the sexual encounter as possible. Part of a SANEs job is to reconstruct the events in question, and evidence collection is typically used in four potential ways:

1. To identify you, the suspect;
2. To document recent sexual contact;
3. To document force, threat, or fear; and

---

[22] Rape, Abuse, and Incest National Network. https://www.rainn.org/about-rainn.
[23] International Association of Forensic Nurses. https://www.forensicnurses.org/page/aboutSANE.
[24] A National Protocol for Sexual Assault Medical Forensic Examinations, Second Edition. United States Department of Justice. https://www.ncjrs.gov/pdffiles1/ovw/241903.pdf.
[25] I.D.

4. To corroborate the facts of the alleged assault.[26]

Once the evidence is collected, the SANE will place the evidence in the Sexual Assault Evidence Collection Kit. Many jurisdictions have developed their own sexual assault evidence collection kits.[27] Typically, the kit will consist of the accuser's clothing; foreign material found on the accuser's body, including blood, dried secretions, fibers, loose hairs, vegetation, soil/debris, fingernail scrapings, hair cuttings, material dislodged from the accuser's mouth, and swabs of suspected semen and saliva from areas highlighted by alternate light sources; vaginal swabs; anal swabs; oral swabs; and body swabs.[28] Once the exam is completed and the evidence is collected, the kit will be sent to a laboratory such as the U.S. Army Criminal Investigation Laboratory (USACIL).[29]

SAFEs can be tremendously helpful to your case. Your attorney must make sure that she has all the evidence collected by the SANE. This includes not just the SANE's notes but also any pictures the SANE took. Your attorney needs to thoroughly comb through each line and word of the SAFE results. Over the years, I have won sexual assault trials based on inconsistencies found in the SAFE results. Be prepared also for the prosecutor to call the SANE who conducted your accuser's exam to testify. Your attorney may want to request a SANE to help in your case. A thorough and precisely executed cross-examination of a Government's SANE witness is second only to the cross examination of your accuser in importance and can be the difference between winning and losing.

After interviewing the accuser and recommending that she consent to a SAFE, law enforcement will likely move on to inter-

---

[26] L. Ledray, SANE Development and Operation Guide, 2000, pg. 79.
http://www.ojp.usdoj.gov/ovc/publications/infores/sane/saneguide.pdf.
[27] A National Protocol for Sexual Assault Medical Forensic Examinations, Second Edition. United States Department of Justice.
https://www.ncjrs.gov/pdffiles1/ovw/241903.pdf.
[28] American College of Emergency Physicians Evaluation and Management of Sexually Assaulted or Sexually Abused Patient, 1999, pp. 101-107.
[29] https://www.cid.army.mil/dfsc-usacil/html#sec3.

viewing witnesses. It is not uncommon for sexual assault cases to be purely based on "he said, she said" evidence. In that case, law enforcement will want to speak with every person your accuser spoke to about the event. Their hope is to find an outcry witness. An outcry witness is the first person who your accuser spoke with about the sexual assault allegation made against you.[30] What your accuser tells an outcry witness may be admissible in trial against you.[31]

In addition to interviewing witnesses, law enforcement officers will be working to collect or seize evidence. Military law enforcement officials have many options when it comes to how they collect evidence, including asking you to produce evidence. Never, ever, consent to turn over any evidence to law enforcement officials before talking to an attorney.

Typically, the most important evidence in a sexual assault case will be the cell phones of both you and your accuser. A federal law enforcement officer, including OSI, NCIS, CGIS, or CID, can request that the military judge issue a warrant or an order for electronic evidence.[32] In order to convince a judge to issue an order for a third party to turn over electronic communications, the officer must show the military judge that probable cause exists to believe that the information sought contains evidence of a crime.[33] To accomplish this, the law enforcement officer must provide to the military judge an affidavit or sworn testimony. Based on that evidence, the judge determines whether probable cause exists to execute the warrant or order.[34]

Again, law enforcement officials are not interested in helping you or corroborating your side of the story. They will typically only try to subpoena or obtain evidence that aligns with or corroborates your accuser's account of the incident. If your

---

[30] "Outcry Witness Law and Definition." USLegal, Inc. Retrieved 13 July 201.
[31] Military Rule of Evidence 803(3) – Excited Utterance.
[32] R.C.M. 703A. Warrant or Order for Wire or Electronic Communications.
[33] R.C.M. 703A(b)(1)(A)-(B).
[34] 18 U.S.C. (§) 2703.

accuser tells law enforcement that you sent her text messages apologizing for what happened the night before, they will do everything to obtain those messages. If you tell them that your accuser sent you nude photos the night before—a fact that may very well help your case—do not bet on law enforcement going out of their way to obtain those messages. If you know there is helpful evidence out there, talk to an attorney as soon as possible and request that your attorney file a preservation request on your behalf. I will talk more about preservation requests in the next section of this book. For now, please, do not rely on CID or OSI to help you obtain favorable evidence. It simply will not happen.

The Role of Your Attorney – Investigate!

I cannot put this more clearly: Do not rely on law enforcement to conduct the investigation for you. I will say it again: Do not rely on law enforcement to conduct the investigation for you! The system is not fair. CID, NCIS, or OSI are not there to help you. CID, OSI, and NCIS only collect the evidence that they need to close their investigation under a probable cause standard. You do not want the law enforcement investigators to be the only people determining what is and what is not relevant. Your attorney has several tools to ensure that your rights are upheld during the investigation stage of the case. Your attorney can accomplish this through filing preservation requests, submitting subpoenas to the trial counsel, and utilizing Article 46 of the UCMJ, which states that you will be granted equal access to witnesses and evidence.

Remember, your attorney is there to help you. Your attorney is there to discover the truth. If you decide to hire an attorney prior to preferral of charges, make sure that the contract you sign to retain that attorney's services has a provision that states: "retainer fee includes pre-preferral investigation. This includes interviewing witnesses, filing a preservation request (if necessary), and filing a notice of representation with command and law enforcement."

It is important to understand that your attorney cannot interfere with a federal law enforcement investigation. Witnesses may not wish to speak with your attorney, and you have no right to discovery at this point in the proceedings. However, there is no rule preventing your attorney from talking to willing witnesses, taking statements, and even conducting a background check on your accuser. One of the first things I do when retained in a sexual assault case is to request that my staff track the accuser on social media. You would be amazed at the things that can be discovered if your attorney follows this principle.

One word of caution: Do not conduct this investigation yourself. You will almost certainly be investigated for obstructing justice or interfering with a lawful investigation. Trust me. If you are accused of sexual assault, you need a professional team. You are not trained to handle this! Again, the nuances of the investigation and pre-preferral procedure are what attorneys are trained to maneuver.

The purpose of a pre-preferral investigation is to build your case early before the military prosecutors start to prepare for trial. Once military prosecutors get involved, witnesses become more hesitant to share their side of the story. Give your attorney a list of witnesses to speak to that may be helpful to your case. Your attorney should be on the prowl to identify prior inconsistent statements made by your accuser and to fully develop any motive your accuser has to fabricate her story against you.[35] Remember, bias, prejudice, and motive to fabricate are always relevant in trial and can be proven by extrinsic evidence.[36]

Motive to fabricate constitutes the single most important part of your defense. If your case ends up in a court-martial, in front of a military judge or a panel, you will be victorious if your attorney identifies a motive to fabricate and builds your case around that motive to fabricate. Your attorney must be prepared

---

[35] Military Rule of Evidence 613 – Witness's Prior Statement.
[36] Military Rule of Evidence 608(c) – Evidence of Bias.

to explain to the panel WHY this woman is on the stand, under oath, and willing to lie. If your attorney can do that effectively, you can win.

To identify and develop that motive to fabricate, your attorney must be conducting witness interviews early and often. Your attorney must also be willing to investigate your accuser's character. He should speak to your accuser's chain of command, supervisors, friends, and ex-boyfriends. Find out if she has made similar allegations in the past or if the people she works with are willing to testify that she is a dishonest person. It is never too soon for your attorney to ask questions to determine whether your accuser is biased or has a motive to hurt you.

Did your accuser have a husband when she messaged you on Tinder? Does your accuser have a mental illness that impacts her ability to process memories accurately? Has your accuser made similar false allegations in the past? You need to know the answers to these questions. Your attorney needs to help you find the answers to these questions.

Even during the pre-preferral stage of the case, your attorney can request to interview your accuser. Remember, your accuser may have an attorney assigned to her. If that is the case, your attorney must request to interview her through her special victim's counsel.[37] If your accuser agrees to speak to your attorney, your attorney should have another witness present during the interview. I have won cases based on statements made by the accuser before preferral and before the military prosecutors had a chance to coach her on what to say and how to say it. This is precious time that can make or break your case. But you must be proactive.

In addition to those witness interviews, your attorney should go to the scene of the alleged assault. Your attorney should aim to get there before the military prosecutor. It helps if your attorney picks a day when the weather and lighting are similar to the time of the alleged assault. Ask your attorney to bring a camera, tape measurer, or video recorder. In some cases, you may want to go

---

[37] Article 46(b), Uniform Code of Military Justice.

with your attorney to the scene. This is a very good opportunity for your attorney to become more familiar with the facts and to possibly spot something that can help you diminish the credibility of your accuser's story.

One important thing to know is that military defense attorneys do not have subpoena power in courts-martial. This can be a major disadvantage if your attorney does not fully understand the tools she has to obtain favorable evidence for you early in the investigation. This is especially true with electronic evidence such as text messages. Most folks think that things really cannot be deleted from a phone. That is not true. Message content on phones is easy to delete, and once deleted, can disappear forever if enough time passes. Most phones will rewrite over deleted content. Once the evidence is gone or no longer exists, the military prosecutors will be relieved of their responsibility to turn that evidence over.

Your attorney has several avenues to ensure that favorable electronic evidence is preserved, collected, and turned over in your case. Your attorney has the power to request an investigative subpoena in your case before or after the referral of charges.[38] With an investigative subpoena, your attorney can obtain evidence not already in the possession, custody, or control of law enforcement.[39]

Your attorney will typically submit the subpoena to the trial counsel.[40] The investigative subpoena is an essential tool for your attorney to use if your accuser's phone has evidence helpful to your case. Maybe your accuser took pictures of the two of you together the night before, and you want those pictures to help corroborate your version of the case. Important, right? Photos and texts are especially important if she tells law enforcement that she gave you no reason to believe she was interested in sex.

In addition to requesting that evidence be subpoenaed, your attorney can request that electronic evidence on your accuser's phone be preserved under the Stored Wire and Electronic

---

[38] R.C.M. 703(g)(3)(C).
[39] I.D.
[40] Army Regulation 27-10, para. 5-16.d(2).

Communications and Transactional Records Access Act.[41] This statute governs all stored wire and electronic communications, including text messages.[42] Pursuant to this statute, your attorney can make a preservation request to the government.

This preservation request will not force the carrier to turn over the evidence, but it will notify the prosecutor that you want this evidence preserved. In this request, your attorney should specifically require that trial counsel and law enforcement send a preservation request specifically to the carrier themselves upon receipt. Your attorney can send a preservation request directly to the carrier, but the request will carry more weight if it comes from the government. Filing preservation requests early and often is key. If the government does not preserve these records, you may be entitled to relief, which could lead to an array of good outcomes for you, like a dismissal of charges.

The Takeaway

If you've been accused of sexual assault, here's what you can expect during the pre-preferral period:

- You will be "flagged." This means your career will be put on hold while the charges against you are investigated and tried.
- You may be placed under some form of pretrial restraint, and will likely be ordered not to make contact with your accuser.
- You might be apprehended and confined. You are entitled to challenge the confinement order within seven days from the date of issue.
- Your accuser will be interviewed by law enforcement. She may also undergo a sexual assault forensic examination (SAFE).

---

[41] 18 U.S.C. (§)(§) 2701-12. See also, U.S. Army Trial Defense Service Deskbook, 3d Edition, October 2016, Ch. 8, Preservation of Evidence and Spoliation.
[42] I.D.

- Law enforcement is likely to subpoena electronic records, including text messages between you and your accuser.
- Your attorney will interview witnesses and examine the evidence collected by law enforcement.

The pre-preferral period is the time to start building your defense. Do not attempt to investigate the allegations against you by yourself, and don't rely on law enforcement's investigation either. Make sure you have an experienced attorney who can ask the right questions and gather relevant information.

Preferral of Charges

Chapter 2

The pre-preferral period ends when you are officially charged with a crime. Once you have been notified of the charges, your battalion and brigade commanders will determine whether to dismiss the charges, remand them to your immediate commanding officer, or take them to trial in a summary, special, or general court-martial.

Preferral of charges is the process whereby you are officially charged with a court-martial offense in the military. Technically, any person subject to the code may prefer charges, but typically your commander will be the person who prefers the charge against you.[43] The person preferring the charge against you must sign the charge sheet under oath before a commissioned officer of the armed forces who is authorized to administer oaths. A judge advocate usually accomplishes the process. The judge advocate is typically the legal

---

[43] R.C.M. 307. Preferral of Charges.

advisor for the commander who is preferring the charges against you. The judge advocate will administer the oath to your commander. Your commander will make the oath and then prefer the charges.

As part of the oath, your commander must swear that he/she has personal knowledge of, or has investigated, the matters outlined in the charges and that those matters, to the best of their knowledge, are true.[44] This is important because the preferral will be defective if your commander does not know the facts of your case and so cannot satisfy this provision. I have filed for dismissal of charges based on commanders who prefer charges not having any information about the case. I have also had a case where the preferring officer called my client into his office to inform him that he did not believe that my client was guilty. I filed a defective preferral motion because part of the oath states that the preferring authority must believe that the matters set forth in the charges are true.

Your commander has broad discretion in deciding which charges they will prefer against you.[45] Typically, once your commander has decided to prefer charges, he has already decided that a court-martial is the proper forum to decide your case. However, the final decision as to whether your case will be sent to trial and what level of court will hear your case is left to your brigade or battalion commander, who possesses prosecutorial discretion in your case.[46]

You Must Be Given Notice of Charges

As the accused, you have the right to be notified of the charges against you.[47] The purpose of this requirement is to ensure that you are given notice of the impending criminal process in

---

[44] R.C.M. 307(b)(1).

[45] Military Criminal Justice Practice and Procedure, Eighth Edition, David A. Schlueter, Chapter, 6-1.

[46] Id.

[47] R.C.M. 308. Notification to accused of charges.

compliance with your due process standards.[48] The rules require that your immediate commander inform you as soon as practicable that charges have been preferred against you, the name of the person who preferred them, and the person who ordered them to be preferred.

Typically, your supervisor will tell you that the commander wants to see you, and you will be told to officially report to that officer at a certain time. In some cases, you may be ordered to report in your dress uniform. You will walk into the room, and your commander, along with his legal advisor, will be sitting there. Sometimes a senior enlisted leader, like your first sergeant, will also be in the room.

From there, your commander will read to you each charge and specification out loud. This is required because you must be informed of the general nature of the charges against you. Once this is complete, you should be given a copy of the charges. At this point, your commander, or the person who gave the notice, will sign item 12 of the charge sheet at the top of page two.

The Charge Sheet

Charges in the military are drafted on DD Form 458, which is used by every branch.[49] The first page is where your personal data is found, whether you endured any pretrial confinement, the charges themselves, and what is known as the preferral section. In this section, your accuser, who is usually the commander, signs and swears he has personal knowledge of the charges or that he has investigated them and that the charges are true.[50]

The second page of DD Form 458 starts with a section notice that you have been notified of the charges. The remaining sections on page two are used for noting receipt of the charges by the summary court-martial convening authority, typically your

---

[48] Id.

[49] Military Criminal Justice Practice and Procedure, Eighth Edition, David A. Schlueter, Chapter, 6-1.

[50] Id.

Preferral of Charges

battalion commander, referring your case to a court-martial, and, lastly, for noting that you have been served a copy of the DD Form 458.[51]

Forwarding the Charges

After the charges are drafted and sworn to, the charges, along with supporting evidence, will be forwarded up through the chain of command.[52] Again, your immediate commander is the person who usually prefers charges and, in doing so, informs you of the charges.[53] Once that happens, the charge sheet, sworn statements, investigator's reports, and other supporting evidence should be forwarded to the next higher level commander, who is normally the summary court-martial convening authority.[54]

In the Army, this is usually your battalion commander. The transmittal form will usually have a place where the commander can make their recommendation as to the type of court-martial that should hear the case. In most of the services, there is also a place where the commander can write a few words about why they have made the recommendation. Your attorney needs to read these recommendations. I have won unlawful command influence motions based on what is written in the forwarding documentation.

Summary Court-Martial Convening Authority

The summary court-martial convening authority will first fill out page two of the charge sheet, which will reflect the time of receipt and initiates the statute of limitations.[55] The statute of limitations is a law

---

[51] Id.

[52] Military Criminal Justice, Practice and Procedure, Eighth Edition, Ch6-2(B), David A Schlueter.

[53] United States v. Gilford, 16 M.J. 578 (A.C.M.R.).

[54] Military Criminal Justice, Practice and Procedure, Eighth Edition, Ch6-2(B), David A Schlueter.

[55] Id; See also Art 43, U.C.M.J.

that forbids prosecutors from charging someone with a crime that was committed more than a specified number of years ago.[56] The main purpose of the statute of limitations is to ensure that convictions are based upon evidence that has not deteriorated with time. After the time period has run, the crime can no longer be prosecuted, meaning that the accused person is essentially free.

The summary court-martial convening authority has several options once he receives the charge sheet. These options include: (1) dismissing the charges; (2) referring the charges to a summary courts-martial; (3) returning the charges to the immediate commander for appropriate action; (4) forwarding the charges with his recommendations to the special court-martial convening authority; or (5) directing that an Article 32 investigation be held if they feel the charges may warrant a general courts-martial.[57]

Special Court-Martial Convening Authority

The special court-martial convening authority is typically your brigade commander. This is also typically the commander who serves in the grade of 0-6 or higher with initial disposition authority for sexual assault cases.[58] This officer's options are generally the same as the summary court-martial convening authority; in actuality, the summary and special court-martial convening authorities may be the same person. The most significant difference is that a special court-martial convening authority has the power to refer your case to a special court-martial.[59]

---

[56] https://criminal.findlaw.com/criminal-law-basics/time-limits-for-charges-state-criminal-statutes-of-limitations.html

[57] Military Criminal Justice, Practice and Procedure, Eighth Edition, Ch6-2(C), David A Schlueter.

[58] See DoD Instruction 6495.02. "Sexual Assault Prevention and Response (SAPR) Program Procedures. March 28, 2013.

[59] Military Criminal Justice, Practice and Procedure, Eighth Edition, Ch6-2(E), David A Schlueter.

General Court-Martial Convening Authority

The general court-martial convening authority is typically a flag officer. This officer has all the same powers as the summary court-martial and special court-martial convening authorities. In other words, the general court-martial convening authority can refer the case to a summary court-martial, special court-martial, or a general court-martial.[60] He can dismiss the charges as well. If he decides to send your case to a general court-martial, he must also do two things: he must order a formal pretrial investigation into the basis of the charges (Article 32 Hearing), and he must be given written pretrial advice from the staff judge advocate.[61]

The Takeaway

- To file charges against you, your commanding officer is required to complete a DD form 458. This officer must swear under oath that he or she believes the charges to be true and accurate.
- You must be notified of the charges specified in the DD form 458 as soon as possible.
- The completed charge sheet, witness statements, and investigators' reports are forwarded up through the chain of command to determine the appropriate type of court-martial for the case.
- Your case will be assigned to a summary court-martial; a special court-martial; or a general court-martial.
- The convening authorities for these types of court-martial also have the authority to dismiss the charges or remand the case back to your immediate superior officer.

---

[60] Military Criminal Justice, Practice and Procedure, Eighth Edition, Ch6-2(E), David A Schlueter.
[61] Id.

The Article 32 Preliminary Hearing

Chapter 3

Sexual assault cases almost always go to a general court-martial. General court-martial cases are required under Article 32 of the UCMJ to include a preliminary hearing. Article 32 hearings determine whether there is probable cause for a charge, or mitigating or extenuating circumstances that should be considered. Both sides in the case may call witnesses or present evidence during the hearing.

If you are accused of sexual assault, you will most certainly face a general court-martial, which means that you are entitled to an Article 32 hearing. Article 32 states that "No charge or specification may be referred to a general court-martial for trial until completion of a preliminary hearing."[62] The official purpose of the Article 32 hearing is to determine the following: (1) whether the charge alleges an offense; (2) whether there is

---

[62] Art. 32(a)(1), UCMJ; R.C.M. 405(a).

probable cause to believe that you, the accused, committed the charged offense; and (3) whether the convening authority has court-martial jurisdiction over you and over the charges you are accused of committing.

There is no judge at an Article 32 hearing. Instead, the case will be assigned to a preliminary hearing officer (PHO).[63] The PHO is most often a judge advocate who is believed to be an impartial officer. This officer is typically an O-3 or O-4 who is not supposed to have any prior knowledge about the case. Typically, the PHO works in the same office as the military prosecutor and works for the same staff judge advocate who recommended that charges be preferred against you. This can be problematic, and your attorney must be aware if the PHO and the trial counsel have a personal relationship.

It may even be appropriate for your defense attorney to question the PHO about his role, his relationship with the trial counsel, or any other issue that may lead to unfairness. A PHO should be disqualified if he or she:

   a. Played a prior role in assembling the case against you;
   b. Previously formed or expressed an opinion about the case against you;[64]
   c. Served as the Deputy Staff Judge Advocate or the Staff Judge Advocate;[65] or
   d. Might be reasonably questioned as to impartiality[66]

The PHO must be a judge advocate if you are charged with sexual assault.[67] The PHO must also be equal or senior in grade to the detailed military counsel for both the government and the

---

[63] Art. 32(b)(1), UCMJ; R.; R.C.M. 405(d)(1).
[64] United States v. Natallelo, 10 M.J. 594 (A.F.C.M.R. 1980).
[65] United States v. Davis, 20 M.J. 61 (C.M.A. 1985).
[66] United States v. Payne, 3 M.J. 354 (C.M.A. 1977)
[67] DA Pam 27-17, para. 1-4b.

defense, if practicable. This rule is designed to ensure that a PHO who may be a captain is not influenced by the rank of a major or lieutenant colonel who is advocating for one side or the other.

If you are accused of sexual assault and face an Article 32 hearing, you do have several rights. You have the right to receive evidence from the government regarding the facts of your case. As soon as practicable but no later than five days after notification of the Article 32 hearing, you have the right to receive the following information/evidence:

a. The Article 32 appointing order;
b. Statements within the control of military authorities of witnesses that the prosecutor intends to call at the hearing;
c. Evidence the prosecutor intends to present at the preliminary hearing; and
d. Any matter provided to the convening authority when deciding to direct or order the preliminary hearing.

Prior to the Article 32 hearing, you also have the right to be given the name and contact information for each witness the prosecutor intends to call at the hearing; any other evidence that the prosecutor intends to offer at the hearing; and any additional information the prosecutor intends to submit within 24 hours after the closure of the hearing. In other words, these rules are designed to ensure that you and your attorney are not caught by surprise during the Article 32 hearing. This sort of ambush is frowned upon, and your attorney should be submitting a discovery request before the Article 32 hearing to ensure that all rules and procedures are followed.

You have additional rights at the hearing itself. These rights include the right to be advised of the charges against you; be represented by counsel; be informed of the purpose of the hearing; be informed of the right against self-incrimination under Article 31; be present throughout the taking of evidence;

cross-examine witnesses on matters relevant to the purpose of the hearing; present matters relevant to the scope of the hearing; and make a sworn or unsworn statement on relevant issues.

One consideration that might arise during an Article 32 hearing is whether there are mitigating or extenuating factors in the case. Mitigating information or evidence in a case, or extenuating circumstances surrounding the commission of an offense, might reduce the severity of the punishment for a crime.[68] Remember, probable cause is based on a totality of the circumstances. One of the PHO's jobs is to determine whether there's probable cause to move forward in the case. The PHO must consider the credibility of the witnesses, which means your attorney can present evidence that would call into question your accuser's credibility. Whether Article 32 is the best place to present this evidence is something that you and your attorney must discuss. Oftentimes, I will not present my best case at the Article 32 hearing. I do not want to give the government the next six months to adjust fire and prepare for its case.

As the accused, you have the right to waive your Article 32 hearing.[69] The right to waive the hearing is a personal right, which means it is your right and your right alone. Your attorney cannot waive the hearing without your informed consent.[70] I typically recommended that my clients waive the Article 32 hearing. First, the probable cause standard is such a low standard that it is very unlikely the PHO will recommend the dismissal of charges. Second, litigating the Article 32 hearing will give the government months and months to fix any issues that your attorney may bring up at the hearing.

In other words, by litigating the hearing, your attorney will be

---

[68] "A matter in mitigation is "introduced to lessen the punishment to be adjudged by the court-martial, or to furnish grounds for a recommendation of clemency." A matter in extenuation "serves to explain the circumstances surrounding the commission of an offense." 73 M.J. 212, 215 n.2 (C.A.A.F. 2014) (quoting R.C.M. 1001(C)(1)(B); see also See also, U.S. Army Trial Defense Service Deskbook, 3d Edition, October 2016, Chapter 6, Article 32 Preliminary Hearings.
[69] Art.32(A)(1), UCMJ; R.C.M. 705(c)(2)(E).
[70] United States v. Garcia, 59 M.J. 447 (C.A.A.F. 2004).

alerting the government to your theory of defense and the weaknesses of the case, and the government will do everything that it can to fix those problems by trial. This is not good. Finally, and most importantly, if the PHO sees uncharged misconduct in the file, he or she can recommend that new charges be preferred.[71] I once had an Air Force Article 32 Hearing where my client walked in with three specifications of sexual assault and walked out with 11! The PHO had recommended that the convening authority prefer eight additional charges of sexual assault. Sad, but true. Do NOT lose the war to win the battle.

In addition to the rights stated above, you have the right to request that the government produce witnesses and evidence. The PHO will set a deadline for your attorney to request witnesses and evidence. That request will be sent to the trial counsel to take action.[72] The trial counsel will either agree to produce the witnesses or reject your attorney's request on the grounds that the testimony offered by the witnesses would be irrelevant, cumulative, and not necessary for the limited scope of the hearing.[73] If the trial counsel objects to your witnesses, which they most certainly will do, the PHO will decide whether the witness is necessary for the purpose of the hearing. Nine times out of ten, the PHO will agree with the government, especially if the witness provided a statement to law enforcement. Unless your attorney can explain why additional testimony from that witness is relevant and necessary to determine whether probable cause exists in the case, the PHO will deny your request for witnesses.

In addition to witnesses, you can also have your attorney request that the trial counsel produces evidence that is helpful to your case at the Article 32 hearing.[74] The trial counsel or prosecutor will either agree to produce the evidence or object to the production of evidence on the grounds that the evidence is

---

[71] R.C.M. 405(e)(2).
[72] R.C.M. 405(g)(1)(A); R.C.M. 405(g)(2)(A).
[73] R.C.M. 405(g)(1)(B).
[74] R.C.M. 405(g)(3)(A)i.

irrelevant, cumulative, or not necessary for the limited purpose of the hearing.[75]

If the government objects and refuses to produce the evidence your attorney requested them to produce, your attorney can request that the PHO make a ruling to settle the matter. If the PHO determines that it is relevant, he will order the trial counsel to produce the evidence. The trial counsel then must make reasonable efforts to obtain the evidence under their control or issue a subpoena duces tecum for defense-requested evidence that is not under their control.[76] This type of subpoena is issued for a third-party entity to produce documents and other tangible evidence.

For example, let us assume that the government has charged you with sexual assault. However, your defense is that you were not at the location of the alleged crime when the assault happened. Instead, you were in an Uber heading to McDonald's for a late-night snack. If the government is not in possession of the Uber records to show that you ordered the Uber at the exact time the complaining witness alleges that she was assaulted, your attorney can request that a subpoena be issued to Uber to produce those documents. These alibi documents would be relevant to the scope of the hearing because there is no probable cause if your attorney can present credible evidence to show that you were not even present when the alleged assault occurred.

Whether to challenge your case at the Article 32 hearing is a decision you must make with your attorney's advice. Understand that there may be many tactical considerations at stake in your case, and your attorney may have a very good reason for not wanting to litigate your case at an Article 32 hearing. Here is my advice: if your attorney requests that you waive the hearing, ask him why and be a good listener. If your attorney has a sound tactical reason for not wanting to contest your case at the Article 32 stage, take her advice. Most PHO's will simply rubberstamp

---

[75] R.C.M. 405(g)(3)(A)(i).
[76] R.C.M. 405(g)(3)(A)(ii).

your case and recommend referral of charges even if you present helpful evidence during the hearing anyway.

Do NOT risk losing the war to win the battle!

The Takeaway

If you've been charged with sexual assault, you're probably facing a general court-martial. The general court-martial will be preceded by a preliminary hearing mandated by Article 32 of the UCMJ.

You have several rights at the Article 32 hearing. These include:

- The right to see the government's evidence against you before the hearing begins, including the names of witnesses.
- The right to be represented by counsel, cross-examine witnesses, and make statements on relevant issues.
- The right to present information regarding mitigating or extenuating factors the court should consider.
- The right to present information that questions the credibility of witnesses or your accuser.
- The right to forego the Article 32 hearing altogether.

Referral of Charges and Convening the Court

Chapter 4

Once charges are referred in your case, the process of assembling the court-martial begins. A military judge, a prosecutor, and a military defense attorney are assigned to the court, and a pool of potential jurors is selected.

The Staff Judge Advocate's Pretrial Advice

Before your case can be referred to a general court-martial, the convening authority must receive advice from his legal officer. Article 34 of the UCMJ requires the convening authority to obtain the formal written opinion of his chief legal advisor.[77] In other words, the staff judge advocate's pretrial advice, along with the Article 32 pretrial investigation, serves as a "screening

---

[77] Military Criminal Justice, Practice and Procedure, Eighth Edition, Ch 7-3(A), David A Schlueter.

device" to ensure that there is probable cause to support the charges and that the charges are in proper form.[78]

The Convening Order

It is important to remember that once the decision is made to refer charges in your case, the convening authority must properly convene and compose the court-martial.[79] Only a properly convened court-martial can hear your case. This means the convening authority's powers are two-fold: the power to appoint the court members and the power to refer your case to a general court-martial. To accomplish this, the convening authority will sign the convening order. The convening order creates the court.[80] The order will clearly state the type of court-martial being formed and names of the court members.

Referral of Charges

When service members call my office, they often ask me to explain the courts-martial process to them. I tell them that referral of charges occurs when the convening authority sends their case to the military judge. This answer is a little simplistic but accurately reflects the point of the process known as a referral. I also point out that referral of charges triggers their right to discovery as well, which will even the playing field. Charges are officially referred against you by the direction of the convening

---

[78] The staff judge advocate is required to include specific information in their advice to the convening authority. This includes: (1) conclusion with respect to whether each specification alleges an offense under the code; (2) conclusion with respect to whether the evidence warrants the allegation of each offense; (3) conclusion with respect to whether a court-martial would have jurisdiction over the offense; and (4) recommendation of the action taken by the convening authority. Id.

[79] Runkle v. United States, 122 U.S. 543 (1886); United States v. Marker, 3 C.M.R. 127 (C.M.A. 1952); Id at Chapter 8-1.

[80] Military Criminal Justice, Practice and Procedure, Eighth Edition, Ch 8-2(C), David A Schlueter.

authority, who will order that a particular court-martial will try your case.[81] The referral of charges is completed when the convening authority or his designee fills out Part V on the second page of your charge sheet.[82]

Again, charges may not be referred to a general court-martial until the convening authority receives the pretrial advice from the staff judge advocate. In determining whether to refer charges against you, the convening authority may rely upon information from any source, whether it be the staff judge advocate or law enforcement.[83] Once charges have been referred against you, you will receive notice, and you will typically sign a notification form. Referral is an informal process and is very different than preferral. Once a case is referred, the power shifts from the convening authority and staff judge advocate to the military judge and the military attorneys. Referral is the process that triggers the litigation period of your case. In other words, referral now means that a military judge and prosecutor will be detailed to your case. Your military defense attorney better be ready to defend you in court.

The Participants

The people who will be participating in your court-martial include the military judge, military counsel or civilian counsel, and the members of the panel.

The Military Judge

The military judge presides over your case during the trial. The military judge must be an attorney who is licensed to practice law in either federal court or the highest court of a state. The military judge must also be certified to perform judicial duties by their

---

[81] See R.C.M. 601(a).
[82] Military Criminal Justice, Practice and Procedure, Eighth Edition, Ch 8-4, David A Schlueter.
[83] R.C.M. 601(d)(1).

judge advocate general.[84] Military judges are not members of the convening authority's command but are usually part of an independent trial judiciary command.[85] In other words, the military justice system must ensure that military judges are free from the influence of your command. This helps to ensure that judges are deciding your case fairly and not to gain favor with your command. Each judge will be attached to a duty station at an installation, or the judge will be a part of a judicial circuit.[86]

Military Counsel

Each general court-martial will almost certainly include one detailed trial counsel and one detailed defense counsel. The trial counsel is the military prosecutor who will be seeking to convict you in the case. It is very common for each general court-martial to consist of an assistant trial counsel and an assistant defense counsel. In a general court-martial, both the detailed trial counsel and defense counsel must be certified under Article 27(b) of the UCMJ by the judge advocate general.[87] At a minimum, this means that your trial defense or area defense attorney must be a member of the highest court of a state or a member of a federal bar.[88]

If you face charges at a general court-martial, you will have the right to appointed free counsel. These counsels are military officers qualified under Article 27(b) to assist you in your case. In the Army, these counsels are referred to as trial defense services officers, and in the Air Force, they are referred to as area defense officers. I have a very high opinion of the defense bar within the military branches. Most of these attorneys are incredibly smart, talented, and hard working. I have only worked with a few over

---

[84] Article 26, U.C.M.J.; See also Military Criminal Justice, Practice and Procedure, Eighth Edition, Ch 8-3(B), David A Schlueter.
[85] Id.
[86] Id.
[87] R.C.M. 502(d)(1).
[88] Article 27(b), U.C.M.J.; See also Military Criminal Justice, Practice and Procedure, Eighth Edition, Ch 8-3(C), David A Schlueter.

the years who were not dedicated to their clients. These counsels will be detailed to your case. Each military defense counsel is detailed in accordance with the service regulations of their specific branch. For example, trial defense attorneys in the Army are detailed by the Chief of the U.S. Army Trial Defense Services or his delegate.[89]

You may also specifically request a military defense attorney to represent you. There may be a military defense attorney you have heard of or who helped a friend of yours out. You can make a specific request for that officer. This is called a request for an individual military counsel or an IAC request.[90] However, that officer will only be appointed to you if they are "reasonably available."[91] I sometimes recommend that my clients request a specific military defense attorney I have worked with in the past. Remember, you are entitled to a military defense attorney even if you hire a civilian, and I will want to make sure that you have the best team possible.

Civilian Counsel

You always have the right to hire civilian counsel. The Manual for Courts-Martial states that you may hire a civilian counsel "if provided at no expense to the government."[92] Once you hire a civilian attorney, UCMJ Article 38 states that your assigned military defense attorney becomes second chair on the case unless excused by you. In other words, the assigned military counsel remains a part of the team. This is very important to understand. I always want the assigned military attorney to remain a part of the team. These officers know the local landscape and can serve a very valuable purpose in the case. If you are accused of sexual assault, you will need a great team to help you out. There is no reason to release your military attorney just because you have

---

[89] Id at Chapter 8-3(C)(2).
[90] Article 38(b)(3), Uniform Code of Military Justice
[91] See Article 38(b)(3), Uniform Code of Military Justice
[92] R.C.M. 506(a)

hired a civilian attorney. However, the civilian attorney becomes the lead on the case and should be the primary litigator at trial.

The Military Jury

A military jury is called a panel. The convening authority is instructed to select panel members who are the "best qualified for the duty by reason of age, education, training, experience, length of service, and judicial temperament."[93] Each panel member must be on active duty; commissioned officers may serve as court members in any case; warrant officers may serve in any case other than the one where the accused is a commissioned officer; enlisted personnel are eligible to serve if the accused has the requested that enlisted members be appointed, and the enlisted members are not in the accused's unit; and if it can be avoided, no member should be junior in rank or grade to the defendant.[94]

Not every panel member selected by the convening authority will sit as a panel member in your case. I will discuss voir dire in more detail later in this book, but understand that once your court-martial starts, your attorneys will begin the process of selecting from that group of service members the best panelists to judge your case. The convening authority may select 20 potential panelists for a court-martial, but only eight will sit as actual jurors during your case. The others will be excused for various reasons after the voir dire process. The convening authority simply selects the service members that your attorney must choose from during voir dire.

The selection process typically consists of the convening authority personally selecting individuals whose names appear in a pool of potential members compiled by his legal staff.[95] However, it is not appropriate for the military prosecutor to be a part of this process. I served as a military prosecutor for several

---

[93] Military Criminal Justice, Practice and Procedure, Eighth Edition, Ch 8-3(D), David A Schlueter.
[94] Id.
[95] Id.

years, and never once did I have any input or knowledge in who the convening authority selected as potential jurors. The senior member of the panel is automatically the president of the court, which is the same thing as a jury foreman.

The Takeaway

Once charges are referred in your case, the convening authority will issue an order to assign the case to a particular court. The convening authority and the staff judge advocate will be out of the picture from this point forward; all other matters related to your case will be handled by the court.

The court-martial consists of:

- *The military judge.* The trial judge usually belongs to an independent judiciary command.
- *A detailed trial counsel.* The is the prosecutor in the case. He or she will argue that you should be convicted of the charges against you.
- *A detailed defense counsel.* A qualified military defense attorney will be detailed to your case for free. You have the right to request a specific military defense attorney.
- *A military panel.* This is the pool of potential jurors at your trial. Neither the prosecutor nor the defense attorney have any say in assembling this pool.
- *Civilian defense counsel.* You may hire a civilian attorney to defend you at your own expense. The civilian attorney and the detailed military attorney would defend you as a team, with the civilian acting as lead.

Initial Appearance and Arraignment

Chapter 5

Your first appearance before the military judge will be at the arraignment hearing. This is a brief hearing where the participants in the case are introduced, the charges verified, and administrative or procedural matters resolved. Panel members are not present at the arraignment. Arraignment usually takes place at least five days after the referral of charges.

Once your case has been referred, you will make your initial appearance before the military judge, and you will likely be arraigned. The initial appearance is usually referred to as an Article 39(a) pretrial session.[96] This pretrial session is only called to resolve administrative and preliminary matters in your case. The hearing is also where the judge ensures that you understand your various trial rights. Your plea of guilty or not guilty is sometimes taken at this hearing. Typically, the

---

[96] See Art. 39(a), U.C.M.J.

hearing lasts no more than 10-15 minutes. The military judge presides over the hearing, but the panel members are not there.

At the hearing, the military judge could technically address any trial issue that may affect your case. According to military justice scholar David A. Schlueter, at a minimum the judge will certainly address the following:

1. Calling the court to order.
2. Announcing the convening orders and referral of charges.
3. Accounting for the parties present and absent.
4. Noting whether the court reporter is present.
5. Announcing the detail and qualifications of the prosecution counsel.
6. Announcing the detail and qualifications of the defense counsel.
7. Explanation of your rights to counsel.
8. Administering any necessary oaths.
9. Stating the general nature of the charges.
10. Announcing the detail of the military judge.
11. Inquiring into grounds for challenge to the military judge.
12. Inquiring into any request for trial by judge alone.
13. Inquiring into any request for enlisted members on the court.
14. Arraignment.[97]

Understanding Your First Appearance

When you first step foot into the courtroom, you will sit with your defense counsel at the defense bar. The military judge will sit on his bench in front of you, the court reporter will be next to the judge, and the prosecutor will likely be sitting 10 feet away

---

[97] Military Criminal Justice, Practice and Procedure, Eighth Edition, Ch 12-1, David A Schlueter.

from you on your immediate right. The gallery where people sit will be behind you, and the panel box, which will be empty, is likely to your right or left.

Once you are seated, the military judge will call the session to order. A bailiff in the room will announce, "all rise" when the military judge enters. Everyone in the room will stand at attention and sit down once the military judge gives the order to be seated. Once that happens, the judge will call the hearing to order. In most sexual assault cases, this initial session will happen at least five days after the referral of charges.

Once the hearing is called to order, the military prosecutor will announce the convening order. He will state that charges have been properly referred, and he will state that you have been properly served with a copy of the charges.[98] From there, the military prosecutor will spell out the name and rank of the parties present in the courtroom. There will be a court reporter in the courtroom as well. The court reporter's job is to keep a verbatim record of the proceedings.[99] The trial counsel will announce his appointment for the record. The military prosecutor will also announce that all members of the prosecution team are qualified under Article 27(b) and state whether they have been previously sworn under Article 42(a), UCMJ.[100]

Once the military prosecutor states her detailing on the record, the defense counsel will make a similar announcement. Your military defense counsel will indicate who detailed her and any assistant defense counsel to the case.[101] If your civilian counsel is present for the arraignment, he will also announce to the military court that he is licensed to practice law and that he has not acted in any manner that would disqualify him from the case. Once this happens, the military judge will then advise you of your right to

---

[98] Id at 12-2(C)
[99] R.C.M. 1103.
[100] Military Criminal Justice, Practice and Procedure, Eighth Edition, Ch 12-2(F), David A Schlueter
[101] Id.

counsel.[102] The military judge will ask you whether you understand those rights, and ask you who you wish to be represented by. You will state your attorneys' names for the record. After that, the military judge will announce that all counsel appears to possess the required qualifications.[103]

The military judge then will administer the oath to any party who is required to take the oath. From there, the military judge will ask you a series of questions concerning your right to trial by judge alone or trial by jury. You have a choice: you can waive your right to trial by members and select trial by judge alone.[104] If you are an enlisted member, you also have the option of electing that at least 1/3 of your panel is enlisted.[105] During this initial session before the military judge, you may also request to defer forum selection until any time before assembly of the court.[106] I almost certainly prefer my client to defer selecting forum during this first appearance before arraignment. Forum selection is a very important part of the process, and at this point in your case, your attorneys have not likely been given all the evidence, and the judge has not ruled on any motions. It is far wiser to wait on forum selection until after your attorney has received, reviewed, and mastered the evidence. Moreover, a judge's ruling on a motion may play a big role in deciding what type of forum to select in your case.

---

[102] R.C.M. 901(d)(4).
[103] Military Criminal Justice, Practice and Procedure, Eighth Edition, Ch 12-2(G)(5), David A Schlueter.
[104] Article 16, U.C.M.J.
[105] Article 25, U.C.M.J.
[106] Military Criminal Justice, Practice and Procedure, Eighth Edition, Ch 12-3(B), David A Schlueter.

Arraignment

The last major item the military judge will cover during your initial appearance is the arraignment.[107] During the arraignment, which will typically be part of your initial appearance, the military judge will announce that you will be arraigned. Trial counsel will provide all parties in the case with a copy of the charge sheet and will ask you on the record whether you wish to have the charges read. You will waive this right, trial counsel will announce that the charges were properly sworn to before a commissioned officer, and at last the military judge will ask you whether you plead guilty or not guilty.[108] Again, I advise my clients to wait to plead guilty or not guilty until after I have had the ability to thoroughly review the evidence and submit motions before the court. There is no reason to enter a plea this early in the case, even if we all know you will plead not guilty. It is better to defer that decision until your attorney has addressed all legal issues in your case. It is important to get arraigned as soon as that five-day waiting period is up. Once you have been arraigned, the prosecutor cannot add additional charges to the charge sheet. The entire initial appearance and arraignment may last 10-15 minutes. As a civilian counsel, I seldom appear at these hearings. I have never felt that my client should pay for me to appear, say nothing of value, and leave.

The Takeaway

The arraignment hearing is usually only 10-15 minutes long and deals primarily with administrative matters. It take place at least five days after the referral of charges. The judge detailed to the case presides over the hearing, but potential panelists are not present.

Your role at the arraignment hearing is the following:

---

[107] Military Criminal Justice, Practice and Procedure, Eighth Edition, Ch 12-4, David A Schlueter.
[108] Id.

- The main purpose of the hearing is to make sure you understand the charges against you and your rights at trial. If you do not, say so.
- You will be given the opportunity to waive your right to trial by jury or, if you are enlisted, to request that at least 1/3 of your panel is also enlisted.
- You may request that the choice of venue for the trial (the forum selection) be postponed until your attorney has had a chance to review the evidence in the case.
- The judge will ask you whether you plead guilty or not guilty, but you do not have to enter any plea at this stage. You can defer pleading until all the legal issues in your case have been addressed.
- Once you have been arraigned, no further charges can be added to your charge sheet.

Your Right to Discovery

Chapter 6

In the discovery phase of a trial, the prosecution provides the defense team with the evidence it plans to use to make its case. This includes the names of witnesses and any evidence that might undermine the credibility of those witnesses or prove your innocence. The reason for this sharing of information is so that the trial proceeds fairly and smoothly.

What is Discovery and Why is it Important?

Discovery is the part of the case where you, the accused, can obtain information possessed by the military prosecutor in your case. The military prosecutor has certain rights to obtain the evidence that your attorney has in his possession as well. This exchange of information is commonly referred to as discovery, which typically occurs before the trial. As evidence surfaces, the discovery phase may extend well after the motions hearing and may not end until the day before trial. I have had cases where the prosecutor was forced to turn over evidence during the trial itself.[109]

At its most basic level, discovery, from the defense point of view, is really about obtaining the evidence that the military prosecutor intends to use against you at trial or obtaining evidence that may be helpful to you at trial. This evidence may include:

   a. Crime scene evidence such as photographs, drawings, or other forensic evidence obtained by law enforcement;
   b. Witness names, law enforcement officers' credentials, and statements made by the different witnesses;
   c. CID, NCIS, or OSI reports, oral testimony from witnesses, scientific reports, and DNA evidence;
   d. Any medical evidence such as reports from treating physicians like the SAFE Nurse.

Why Do We Have Discovery?

The discovery process is all about making sure that your attorney is not ambushed at trial when presented with evidence the government intends to use to incriminate you. The military has a tradition of open discovery that is really designed to promise fairness and efficiency in the courtroom.[110] In other words, the

---

[109] "If, before or during the courts-martial, a party discoveries additional evidence or material previously requested or required to be produced, which is subject to discovery or inspection under this rule, that party shall promptly notify the other party or the military judge of the existence of the additional evidence or material." U.S. Army Trial Defense Service Deskbook, 3d Edition, October 2016, Chapter 7: Discovery and Disclosure; see *United States v. Eshalomi*, 23 M.J. 12 (C.M.A. 1986).

[110] "Military legal practice is often characterized by open and free discovery of the government's case by the defense. Such discovery may be far more liberal than that required by law."[110] U.S. Army Trial Defense Service Deskbook, 3d Edition, October 2016, Chapter 7: Discovery and Disclosure. See also Francis A.

purpose of discovery is to ensure that you have all of the information in the government's possession that it either intends to use against you during its case or that may help you formulate your defense.

Understand that if the discovery phase is working as designed, the government should not deny your attorney the ability to obtain evidence that is helpful in your case. However, understand this as well: many military prosecutors do not understand that the discovery process is designed to promote fairness, and they will attempt to play games with your attorney. Your attorney must use all the tools he has at his disposal to force the government to do the right thing. The very best prosecutors I have worked against turn over everything they are supposed to turn over and eliminate gamesmanship from the process.

The Root of Your Discovery Rights

Article 46 of the Uniform Code of Military Justice is the root source for your discovery rights during the criminal process, and this rule promotes open discovery. The rule is simple: "The trial counsel, the defense counsel, and the court-martial shall have equal opportunity to obtain witnesses and other evidence," and "Each party shall have adequate opportunity to prepare its case and equal opportunity to interview witnesses and inspect evidence. No party may unreasonably impede the access of another party to a witness or evidence."[111]

The military rules that deal with discovery focus on ensuring that each party has equal access to evidence so that the defense can prepare its case and to promote efficiency in the process. To this point—and this is important to understand—the rules of discovery do not focus exclusively on evidence that would be

---

Gilligan & Frederic I. Ledereer, Court Martial Procedure & 11-10.00 (3rd ed. 2006).

[111] U.S. Army Trial Defense Service Deskbook, 3d Edition, October 2016, Chapter 7: Discovery and Disclosure; see also R.C.M. 701(e).

admissible at trial only.[112] In other words, if the evidence that you seek can assist your attorney in preparing your defense, it does not necessarily have to be admissible in trial.[113]

How the Process Works

The exchange of evidence is, typically, a rather easy process. Shortly after charges are referred against, your attorney will submit what is known as a discovery request. This is a document that spells out all the evidence, materials, and information your attorney believes the government must turn over in your case. This request is typically generic and basically asks the government to turn over all evidence relevant to your case that is within its possession and control. This includes all information collected or obtained by the law enforcement agency working your case along with any evidence the convening authority would have seen when deciding to refer your case.

If there is evidence that you or your attorney wish the government to turn over that is not within their control or possession, your attorney may need to request that information specifically. First, the government must know the evidence exists, and second your attorney must explain how the evidence is relevant to your case preparation.

For example, let us assume that you have told your attorney that your accuser texted you several nude photos of herself before she came over to your house, which led to the sexual encounter that now serves as the basis of your charge sheet. If your accuser never informed law enforcement that she sent you text messages

---

[112] See United States v. Stone, 40 M.J. 420, 422 (C.M.A. 1994); see also U.S. Army Trial Defense Service Deskbook, 3d Edition, October 2016, Chapter 7: Discovery and Disclosure

[113] "An accused's right to discovery is not limited to evidence that would be known to be admissible at trial. It includes material that would assist the defense in formulating a defense strategy." United States v. Luke, 69 M.J. 309 (C.A.A.F. 2010); U.S. Army Trial Defense Service Deskbook, 3d Edition, October 2016, Chapter 7: Discovery and Disclosure

and you exercised your right to remain silent, the government may not have a clue that this helpful evidence exists. So, your attorney will need to request that the government preserve, subpoena, and produce those text messages. (The process is not quite this simple, but you get the point.) There are some cases where your attorney can request that the military judge sign a warrant for electronic communications shared between you and your accuser. Your attorney needs to explain to the government or the judge why the evidence is relevant and necessary to prepare the case.

If the government denies your attorney's request to turn over certain pieces of information, your attorney can seek relief from the military judge, who can order the government to turn over the evidence. We discuss motions practice in the next chapter; for now, it is important to understand that your attorney can seek relief from the military judge. If your attorney does file a motion to compel the government to produce evidence, your attorney must be prepared to argue why the evidence is necessary and relevant. As an example, I once had a sexual assault case at Fort Stewart, GA. My client was accused of abusive sexual contact. During witness interviews, I discovered that the accuser hated being in the Army and complained about her job all of the time, and shortly after making this allegation against my client, requested a medical separation from the military due to the assault. I also discovered that shortly after her separation, she applied for veteran's assistance and was receiving a tax-free check each month from the VA.

I requested that the government subpoena the VA records and turn over the accuser's separation documents. The government turned over the separation documents but refused to subpoena the VA records, claiming that the evidence was outside their possession and control. I filed a motion with the military judge, argued why the evidence was necessary for the preparation of our defense, and called an expert on the VA claims process to explain what evidence was likely in the possession of the VA. The military judge agreed with my argument and ordered the government to produce the evidence. Ultimately, the accuser decided that she no longer wished to testify, and the charges were dropped.

Evidence the Government Must Disclose No Matter What

There are certain pieces of evidence or types of information that the government must turn over without a request from you. This evidence includes any papers that accompanied the charge sheet when the convening authority referred your case, the convening orders that sent your case to a courts-martial, and any signed or sworn statements in possession of the government that directly relate to the offense you are charged with.[114] The rules want to make sure that the process is fair and fairness dictates that no matter what, this evidence must be provided to you and your attorney. You should receive this evidence shortly after charges are referred against you.

In addition to the evidence listed above, and before the beginning of trial, the government must notify you of the names and addresses of the witnesses the government intends to call to incriminate you at trial.[115] Again, the system is designed to promote fairness and avoid ambush, which means you and your attorney must know who the government is calling during their case, and your attorney must interview each one of these witnesses before trial.

Before your arraignment, the military prosecutor must also notify your attorney if they intend to use any prior criminal conviction you may have had in your past.[116] This rule is also designed to prevent surprise or ambush at trial. It is seldom issued in a military sexual assault case because most service members have never been convicted of a crime relevant to a sexual assault courts-martial. It's rare to see someone enlist or commission if they have a criminal record that would include

---

[114] R.C.M. 701(a)(10.
[115] R.C.M. 701(a)(3).
[116] R.C.M. 701(a0(4).

crimes relevant to a sex assault allegation. Nonetheless, the rule is there and if you have a skeleton in your closet, tell your attorney. Knowledge is power.

Evidence the Government Must Disclose Upon Your Request

There are certain pieces or types of evidence that the military prosecutor must give to your attorney whether you ask for that evidence or not. There is also evidence the government does not have to turn over unless your attorney submits a discovery request and asks the government to turn that evidence over. You may ask why an attorney would not request helpful evidence. Well, remember, you and your attorney must turn over certain types of evidence. If your attorney requests that the government turn over documents, your attorney will likely have to turn over documents to the government, and you may not want to give the government helpful evidence in your case.

RCM 701(a)(2) states that upon request, the military prosecutor shall permit your attorney to inspect documents and tangible evidence in the possession, custody, and control of the government and which are either intended for use by the military prosecutor as evidence in their case or material to the preparation of the defense or were obtained from you. This evidence refers to physical evidence such as photographs, drawings, clothes your accuser may have worn during the alleged assault, or text messages your accuser may have sent to others about the alleged assault.

This rule also states that the military prosecutor shall permit the defense to inspect results or reports of physical or mental examinations, and of scientific tests or experiments, which are in the possession, custody, or control of military authorities, and either intended for use by the military prosecutor as evidence in the case-in-chief or material to the preparation of the defense.

Brady Evidence – TURN IT OVER!

In 1963, in Brady v. Maryland, the United States Supreme Court ruled that "the suppression by the prosecution of evidence favorable to an accused upon request violates due process where the evidence is material either to guilt or punishment, irrespective of the good faith or bad faith of the prosecution."[117] RCM 701(a)(6) implements the Court's holding in *Brady* and codifies that certain pieces of evidencemust be turned over in a case.[118]

RCM 701(a)(6) states that the military prosecutor must turnover, as soon as practicable, evidence which reasonably tends to negate guilt; reduce the degree of guilt; reduce the punishment; or adversely affect the credibility of any witness. Evidence that negates guilt is referred to as exculpatory evidence. Exculpatory evidence is evidence that would tend to absolve the accused of guilt.[119] An example would be if the government has a DNA report which shows that someone else was the source of semen on the night your accuser was sexually assaulted. The military prosecutor would have to turn that evidence over no matter what.

When we are talking about evidence that calls into question a witness's credibility, we are typically talking about impeachment evidence.[120] In other words, this is evidence that your attorney can use to show that a government witness is lying, changed her story, or is not telling the truth. This rule means that if the government obtains evidence that one of the witnesses in your case changed her story during witness interviews, the government must turn that evidence over. Variances, or changes in a witness's statement, must be turned over and provided to your attorney.[121] Military prosecutors often do

---

[117] Brady v. Maryland, 373 U.S. 83, 87 (1963).
[118] U.S. Army Trial Defense Service Deskbook, 3d Edition, October 2016, Chapter 7: Discovery and Disclosure.
[119] https://www.law.cornell.edu/wex/exculpatory_evidence
[120] "Impeachment evidence consists of evidence which tends to impeach or contradict a Government witness." United States v. Bagley, 473 U.S. 667, 676-677 (1985). See also [120] U.S. Army Trial Defense Service Deskbook, 3d Edition, October 2016, Chapter 7: Discovery and Disclosure.
[121] *Giglio v. United States*, 405 U.S. 150 (1972)

not understand this rule and argue that the notes they take during witness interviews are attorney work product and thus are not subject to discovery. This is not always accurate. If your accuser changes her story, the government must disclose that change to your attorney.

Last year, in an Army sexual assault case, the accuser initially told CID that she did not exchange sexual text messages with my client before he allegedly assaulted her. A week before trial, the accuser changed her story and admitted to the prosecutor that she did exchange sexual text messages with my client two days before the alleged assault occurred. The military prosecutor was forced to turn over his notes about this material change in the accuser's story. I obviously used this evidence to my advantage during the trial. If there is a change in a witness's story from one statement to the next, the prosecutor must turn that evidence over.

Conclusion – Fight for Discovery and the Production of Documents

Discovery is a very important tool your attorney must use to obtain helpful evidence in your case. Your attorney is only as good as the evidence and the facts in her possession. Tell your attorney everything that you know about the case and be honest. He needs to know what evidence is out there that can hurt or help you. Your attorney needs to be speaking with you weekly about the evidence in his possession, the evidence not yet in his possession, and the evidence he seeks to admit at trial to fight your case. You need to help your attorney understand what evidence is out there—good or bad—and your attorney needs to pester the government if necessary to obtain that evidence. Do NOT count on law enforcement to obtain helpful evidence in your case.

The Takeaway

The discovery phase of a trial is intended to provide both sides with all the information they need to prepare their case.

- Some information must be handed over to the defense automatically. This includes such your charge sheet and other filing documents.
- Other information must be obtained through a written request. This includes the names of witnesses and other kinds of material evidence.
- Some information that could be useful in your defense may not be under the control of the prosecution. Your attorney may have to ask the judge in the case to compel the prosecution to obtain it.

Your defense team will be on the lookout for evidence in the discovery that is either exculpatory or impeachable.

- Exculpatory evidence is evidence that shows that you are not guilty of the crime of which you are accused.
- Impeachment evidence is evidence that undermines the credibility of your accuser or one of the prosecution's witnesses.

The Motions Hearing

Chapter 7

The motions hearing is where your attorneys can lay the groundwork for the trial itself. They may file a motion for evidence to be included in the trial, or eliminated from it. They will have to convince the judge to approve the motion by showing that their argument is legally valid and supported by evidence. You may be advised to testify during the motions hearing.

What is a Motions hearing, and Why is it so Important?

A sexual assault case can be won and lost during a motions hearing. Towards the end of the Civil War, both sides placed a high degree of priority upon prepping the battlefield before the first shot was fired. The South, at Petersburg, was especially active in prepping the battlefield in anticipation of an advance from General Grant and the Army of the Potomac. A motions hearing is your attorney's opportunity to prep the battlefield: to test the government's case, call witnesses, and seek to introduce evidence that, if admitted, will cripple your accuser's credibility. If your attorney does his job well, you should have a very good feel for your case after the motions hearing—good or bad.

A motions hearing date is set by the military judge to determine and decide legal issues before trial. In other words, your attorney will file a motion to the court to settle a legal issue before trial or seek some form of relief from the military judge. For example, perhaps you made a damaging statement to law enforcement that your attorney wants to keep out of the panel's ears. Your attorney will file a motion and ask the judge to determine whether that statement is admissible against you in court. Perhaps you and your accuser were having sex days and weeks before she accused you of sexual assault. Your attorney will likely file a motion under Military Rule of Evidence 412 to admit that evidence before trial. This will help your attorney properly prepare your case and may lead to the preadmission of evidence that will force the government to dismiss their charges.

Motions are often written requests to the military judge to decide a legal issue before trial. A written motion will consist of several different parts or elements:

1. Your attorney will request that the judge grant you a specific type of relief. For example, your attorney will request that certain acts of uncharged misconduct against you be ruled inadmissible or that a statement you made be suppressed.
2. Your attorney will address in writing who has the burden of proof in the motion. If your attorney is the one filing the motion, he will typically have to prove the facts stated in his motion by a preponderance of the evidence, or 51 percent.
3. Your attorney will spell out the facts that support your position.

4. Your attorney will list specific pieces of evidence that should be attached to the motion for the military judge to consider. This evidence is typically considered an enclosure to the motion and must be presented to the military judge. The fact section mentioned in point 3 is not evidence. Those facts must be supported by physical evidence or witness testimony.
5. Your attorney will apply the law to the facts and argue your position. For example, if you are seeking to admit a prior sexual relationship with your accuser to prove that she consented on the night in question, your attorney will call witnesses to testify about your relationship with your accuser, may call your accuser to the stand, or he may even ask you to testify or provide an affidavit.
6. Your attorney will write a conclusion statement again requesting relief.

Litigating Your Motion

Once your attorney files motions with the military judge, the next phase of the motions hearing will be the hearing itself. It works like this: your attorney files a written motion with the court requesting relief; the opposing party responds to that written motion with their own motion, and then both sides will likely argue the motion before the military judge in court. Your attorney will show up, call witnesses, and argue for a specific type of relief.

General Rule of Law. I now want to discuss a few specific points you and your attorney should know when litigating or arguing your motion. Remember, your attorney will file a written motion with the court, which simply addresses the issues to litigate. Most often, you and your attorney will argue the motion in court before the military judge. Again, your attorney will be asking for some form of relief that will help your case, or your attorney will be fighting to keep evidence out that may hurt your case. Keep in mind, this is all about prepping the battlefield before the fight.

The military judge is given broad discretion to decide the legal issues that you raise in your motions. Strictly speaking, this means that the military judge decides whether the evidence you seek to admit is admissible.[122] In making these decisions, military judges are not bound by the rules of evidence except for privileges.[123] In other words, the rules of evidence allow the judge to consider evidence that would otherwise be inadmissible in the trial if he or she finds it relevant to the motions that are being litigated. If the military prosecutor objects to hearsay during the motions hearing, your attorney can simply say the hearsay rules do not apply in a motions hearing. This, as always, will be up to the judge's discretion.

Burden of Proof. The burden of proof, which is your obligation to prove that the facts you allege are true and that those facts support your theory to admit the contested evidence, often lies with the side who filed the motion. If your attorney wants to admit evidence on your behalf, the burden of proof typically lies with you. Generally, there are some exceptions to this, such as an Unlawful Command Influence motion, but, typically speaking, the party who raises the issue has the burden.

Standard of Proof. As discussed briefly above, the most common standard of proof litigated at a motions hearing is a preponderance of the evidence. There are some motions where the standard of proof is clear and convincing evidence, such as consent searches or subterfuge inspections.[124] Under this standard, the burden of proof is met when the party with the burden convinces the fact finder that there is a greater than 50 percent chance the claim or assertion is true.[125] This means that if your attorney is attempting to admit into

---

[122] Military Rule of Evidence 104(a).
[123] Id.
[124] U.S. Army Trial Defense Service Deskbook, 3d Edition, October 2016, Chapter 11: Motions Practice.
[125] Cornell Law School, law.cornell.edu/wex/preponderance_of_the_evidence.

evidence that you and your accuser had sex the day after she claimed you sexually assaulted her, he must prove that the sex occurred by a 51 percent margin. Then he must be able to articulate why the sexual encounter is admissible in court.

Should You Testify at a Motions Hearing? There may be a fact of consequence in your case that only you and maybe your accuser have personal knowledge of. Your accuser is unlikely to admit the fact on the witness stand, so you are the only source of evidence. In this case, I typically request that my client either testify or, more preferably, provide a written affidavit attesting to the fact under oath. Whether you, as the accused, provide testimony at a motions hearing is a decision to make with your attorney. Understand that if you do decide to testify at a motions hearing, you do not, by testifying on a matter in dispute, become subject to cross-examination on other issues in the case.[126] This means that if you testify during a hearing to suppress evidence of a statement that you made to law enforcement, you cannot be cross-examined on any other area of the case that is not directly related to your statement to law enforcement. This is vital for both you and your attorney to understand.

The Biggest Mistake I See Attorneys Make. The written motion is not evidence. The fact section in the written motion is not evidence. Your attorney must offer proof when litigating a motion. If your attorney alleges that your accuser lied about her relationship with you to protect her marriage, your attorney must provide evidence that your accuser was married. She can accomplish this by filing a marriage certificate, calling your accuser to the stand, or calling your accuser's spouse to the stand. Remember, witness testimony is evidence. I see young attorneys make the mistake of failing to admit evidence to support their position all the time. This is a mistake your attorney cannot afford to make. If your motion fails, your case may be doomed.

---

[126] Military Rule of Evidence 104(d).

Conclusion

The motions hearing is the first major appearance you will have on your way to a contested trial. The motions hearing, from a defense perspective, is all about prepping the battlefield. By the time of the motions hearing, your attorney should have already spoken to all the relevant witnesses in your case, and you and your attorney should both have a strong understanding of what your theme and theory of the case is going to be. If, by this point, your attorney has not explained to you how the motions that he intends to file support your theme of the case, there is something wrong. Each motion filed by your attorney should support your theory of the case. This is key.

The Takeaway

The motions hearing is important in setting the framework for the trial itself. Your attorney can file a motion requesting that the judge compel the prosecution to produce specific evidence during the trial, or rule other evidence inadmissible. To convince the judge to rule in favor of the motion, you and your attorney will have to:

- Prove that the facts in your motion are true and relevant. The burden of proof is always on the side that files the motion. Facts must be proved to at least a 51% certainty.
- Produce evidence to support those facts. This evidence may include witness testimony. Your attorney may also advise you to either testify at the hearing or provide a written affidavit on the specific fact in question.

Military Rule of Evidence 412: The Rape Shield Law

The purpose of MRE 412 is to protect rape victims from being portrayed in the trial as "asking for it." The rule says that claims based on the victim's prior sexual conduct, her clothing, or her profession are not admissible in court. There are some exceptions to this rule.

What You Must Know

Military Rule of Evidence 412 is commonly referred to as the rape shield law. The Rule, at its heart, is designed to protect a victim of sexual assault from embarrassing or humiliating evidence of their sexual behavior that is not relevant to the charged offenses. For example, if your accuser is a stripper and you wish to admit into evidence that she takes her clothes off for a living because you think that will make her look bad in front of the panel, chances are that evidence is not going to be admitted. Your attorney must show a connection between the evidence to be admitted and the charged offenses. For example, let us assume that you met your accuser at the strip club, and she gave you lap dances and texted you to call her when you got home. Your attorney can show a connection or a nexus between her being a stripper and the charged offenses. The connection is that you believed, based on her prior behavior, that she consented to sex.

General Rule of Law

MRE 412(a) generally prohibits evidence offered to prove that the alleged victim engaged in other sexual behavior or that the alleged victim has certain sexual predispositions. We will discuss the three primary exceptions to this rule and how to get helpful evidence admitted in your case.

Other Sexual Behavior. Other sexual behavior is basically any sexual behavior your accuser may have engaged in that is not encompassed by the offenses you are charged with.[127] Your accuser may have slept with everybody in your unit, but that does not mean this evidence is going to be admissible. Clients call me all the time and want to talk about how many men or women their accuser has fooled around with. Here is the problem: this information is not relevant to your case. That is, it is not relevant to your case on its own. What does that evidence have to do with you? How is that evidence related to your theory of defense? There is not a judge in the military that will permit your attorney to argue that your accuser is sexually promiscuous and thus could not have been raped. You must find a nexus between her behavior and your charges.

Sexual Predisposition. This term typically refers to aspects of your accuser's mode of dress, speech, or lifestyle that may contain a sexual connotation for the panel.[128] Just because your accuser talks openly about her sexual fantasies does not mean this evidence is admissible, however. You and your attorney must find a

---

[127] M.R.E. 412(d).
[128] M.R.E. 412(d).

nexus or a link between her mode of speech and the offenses you are charged with. We will discuss the exceptions to this rule shortly, but you must know that your accuser's mode of speech or dress cannot be admitted if the evidence is designed solely to make her look like a morally casual person or the type of person who is looking for casual sex. All of this is relatively simple: evidence will not be permitted just to show that your accuser is the type of person to engage in illicit sexual activity. You must find another way to admit this evidence.

Exceptions to the Rule

For almost every rule lawyers learn in law school, there are exceptions. MRE 412 is no different. The exceptions to the rape shield law are based on your constitutional right to a fair defense. For example, what if you and your accuser had sex the day after she alleged that you raped her? What if, hours before your sexual encounter, your accuser sent you a text message explaining how badly she wants you to do "dirty" things to her? What if she is sleeping with another person in your unit and only accuses you of sexual assault after you tell that other person that you and she have been hooking up? All these scenarios are issues litigated under the exceptions discussed below.

The It Was Not Me Exception. MRE 412(b)(1)(A) states that the military judge should admit evidence of specific sexual encounters your accuser may have engaged in to prove that someone other than you was the source of semen, injury, or other physical injuries. Here is a good example: I once had a case where the government charged my client with sexual assault. The prosecutors sought to admit photographs of the accuser that were taken the morning after the accuser told law enforcement that my client sexually assaulted her. We obtained evidence that the accuser was also sexually active with another man and often bragged about her desire for "rough sex."

My paralegal and I interviewed the other man and found out that two days before the accuser hooked up with my client, she had had "rough sex" with him. I filed a motion under MRE 412 to admit this specific sexual encounter to show the panel that the accuser obtained the bruises during her sex with this third party and not my client. Ultimately, the judge agreed with us, and the client was found not guilty.

The "We Have Done It Before" Exception. MRE 412(b)(1)(B) states that a military judge may admit evidence of specific sexual behavior/encounters between you and your accuser to help you prove that your accuser consented to the sex that you have now been charged with. Here is a good example: I once had a client who was accused of sexual assault by a woman that he had been having casual sex with in the months leading up to the charged offense. During the hearing, my client provided an affidavit that indicated how similar their prior sexual acts had been to the charged offense. We informed the military judge that each time they had sex, they both drank alcohol, went from the couch to her bedroom, kissed, performed oral sex on each other, and had intercourse. We presented this evidence to the military judge to show how similar the charged events were to their prior instances of consensual sex. The military judge ultimately admitted this evidence, and my client was found not guilty.

The "I Have a Right To Fight Back" Exception. MRE 412(b)(1)(C) states that the military judge must admit evidence that is relevant, material, and favorable to your defense.[129] This exception is the most litigated and often the most difficult exception for your defense attorney to handle. If you and your attorney are going to be successful, your attorney must focus on explaining to the military judge how the proffered evidence is consistent with your theory of defense at trial.[130] If your attorney can effectively show the nexus between your theory of defense and the evidence you seek to admit, the judge should admit the evidence.

Here is a good example: Last year, I represented an airman who

---

[129] United States v. Ellerbrock, 70 M.J. 314 (C.A.A.F. 2011).

[130] U.S. Army Trial Defense Service Deskbook, 3d Edition, October 2016, Chapter 14: Military Rule of Evidence 412.

was accused of sexual assault. The accuser did not report my client until my client started to brag about hooking up with the accuser while on temporary duty assignment. This was problematic for the accuser because she was married to another airman stationed at the same installation as my client. To make matters worse for this accuser, her husband, just three months before she accused my client of assault, had been caught having an affair with another airman. Her husband threatened to divorce the accuser if she ever had another affair, and he actually attacked the accuser's boyfriend. I filed a motion to admit into evidence that the accuser had a prior sexual relationship with a man that was not her husband and that she was motivated to save her marriage, which led to her false accusation against my client. Ultimately, the military judge allowed us to admit evidence of this prior affair, and my client was found not guilty.

In this case, I was able to directly relate the facts of the affair to our theory of defense—the accuser wanted to save her marriage and so falsely accused my client to avoid her husband finding out the truth. In other words, the accuser had a motive to lie. A good defense attorney must explain to the military judge how the MRE 412 evidence makes it more or less likely that you are guilty of the offenses. Your attorney must be able to connect the MRE 412 evidence you seek to admit to the material issue in the case using an argument to persuade the judge to admit the evidence. Again, your attorney must be prepared to show the military judge that the evidence is relevant, material, and favorable to your theory of defense.

The Takeaway

MRE 412 is known as the rape shield law. Its purpose is to prevent rape victims from being blamed for their own sexual assault, or having potentially embarrassing information revealed at trial if it is unconnected to the charges. This includes the accuser's sexual behavior with other people, the way she dresses or talks, and her lifestyle generally.

There are some exceptions to the MRE 412 rule:

- Proof that someone other than the accused was the source of evidence such as semen or physical injuries.
- Proof that behavior similar to the charged offense was engaged in consensually in the past.
- Proof that your accuser is lying.

Military Rule of Evidence 413: The "He Has Done It Before" Rule

Chapter 9

If you're on trial for sexual assault, and you have been charged with sexual assault in the past, MRE 413 says that the prior assault can be introduced as evidence of a tendency towards this kind of crime. To block the admission of that evidence, your attorney must either show that you were not given proper notice of the prosecution's intent to use it, or that the prior offense does not meet the military's definition of sexual assault.

Generally speaking, the law does not allow the military prosecutors to admit evidence of other bad acts you have committed. MRE 404(a) prohibits the government from offering evidence of your character simply to show that you are the kind of person who breaks the law. However, in sexual assault cases, there is one big exception that allows the government to offer prior bad acts simply to prove that you are the kind of person who would sexually assault someone else.

MRE 413 allows the military judge to admit evidence that you committed another sexual offense into evidence and that evidence may be considered by the panel for any relevant purpose. Here is how it works. Let us say that three years before you were charged with sexual assault, you were charged with assault consummated by a battery because you punched a guy in a bar who poured a beer on your head. The government cannot admit this prior alleged bad act against you in a sexual assault case simply to show that you are the kind of person who breaks the law. Now, let us assume that you were accused of grabbing a woman's breast in that same bar two years earlier. The government may admit evidence of this prior sexual act to show the panel that you are the kind of person who has a propensity to sexually assault women.

General Rule of Law

To admit evidence under MRE 413, the government must satisfy three prongs:

1. That you, the accused, are actually charged with a sexual offense;
2. That the evidence the government seeks to offer is evidence that you committed another sexual offense; and
3. That the evidence the government seeks to offer is relevant to the case.

Even if the government is able to establish by a preponderance of the evidence that all three prongs are met, the military judge may still exclude the prior offense if he feels that the value of that prior offense in the government's case.[131]

---

[131] United States v. Wright, 53 M.J. 476 (C.A.A.F. 2000)

In determining whether or not the government's proposed evidence of a prior offense is outweighed by the dangers of unfair prejudice against you, she will look at several factors:

1. The judge will determine how much proof there is against and the strength of that proof;
2. Whether the evidence, in light of the charged offenses, is helpful to decide a contested point in the trial;
3. Whether the government can admit the evidence against you in a less prejudicial manner;
4. The time that will be needed at trial for the government to prove the other acts;
5. Whether the evidence will distract the panel from the purpose of the trial;
6. How frequently you, the accused, allegedly engaged in the prior acts of sexual misconduct;
7. The presence or lack of intervening circumstances;
8. Your relationship with the woman or man that is accusing you of these uncharged acts;
9. How close in time the charged acts occurred compared to the uncharged acts; and
10. The similarity of the uncharged acts and the charged conduct.[132]

How it Works

Recently, I had a client who was charged with abusive sexual contact. The accuser alleged that my client grabbed her butt in the motor pool without her permission. The government charged my client with abusive sexual contact and alleged that he committed the offense to satisfy his sexual desires.

A few days after my client was charged, I was given MRE 413 notice. Remember, the government must give your attorney prior

---

[132] United States v. Bailey, 55 M.J. 38 (C.A.A.F. 2001; see also Ch. 14 of DCAP Deskbook.

notice of their intent to offer this statement.[133] That notice must include the statement made by your accuser or a summary of your accuser's expected testimony.[134]

The government provided me with a decision from 11 years earlier written by a female who was now a sergeant first class. The allegation made by this accuser was that my client grabbed her butt in her apartment after they had watched a movie. A few days after that notice, I received notice from the government that there were now three additional women from my client's unit who were alleging that he grabbed their butts or breasts in a sexual manner. As you can imagine, my client and I were very concerned about this new evidence.

I immediately filed a motion with the military judge to exclude the evidence and rule that the panel could not hear the evidence. I attacked each allegation independently. As for the SFC, I argued that the charged acts and the uncharged acts were separated by over ten years, and that therefore the probative, or evidentiary, value of the proposed evidence was significantly outweighed by the dangers of unfair prejudice. I also argued that the facts of the charged offenses and the uncharged offenses were not nearly as similar as the government alleged. For the charged offenses, the conduct allegedly took place in a motor pool, the accuser and my client did not have a prior relationship, and, as the government stated, my client was an NCO while the accuser was a junior enlisted. The government argued that my client used his rank to take advantage of the junior enlisted. The uncharged offenses took place while the now SFC and my client were on a date in her apartment, and alcohol was involved, and my client and the SFC were the same rank. Therefore, the government's theory of the case, that my client used his rank to take advantage of his female soldiers improperly, had no bearing on this uncharged allegation.

As for the other three women, I argued that the government could not prove by a preponderance of the evidence that the

---

[133] MRE 413(b).
[134] Id.

uncharged misconduct occurred. The accusers all claimed that my client had touched them on their butts in March 2019 while they were standing in the parking lot. However, I presented orders from my client's Official Military Personnel File that clearly showed he was stationed on another base during March 2019 attending training. Ultimately, the judge ruled that this evidence was not admissible against my client. This was a huge win. Instead of defending against five charges of abusive sexual contact, my client was only defending against two allegations of abusive sexual assault. Yes, much to my dismay, the judge allowed the government to admit evidence of the prior bad act stemming from over ten years ago.

How to Attack MRE 413 Evidence in Court

1. *No Disclosure.* The first thing your attorney must ensure is that the government properly disclosed to you their intent to offer MRE 413 evidence.[135] As stated above, the government is required to provide to your attorney the evidence they seek to admit. Typically, the military judge will issue a pretrial order to lay out the government's deadlines to provide this notification. Your attorney must hold their feet to the fire and object at trial if proper notice was not given.
2. *The Prior Act is Not a Sexual Offense.* The Manual for Courts-Martial (MCM) specifically lays out what is and what is not considered a sexual offense. Your attorney must analyze the alleged uncharged acts carefully and make sure they fall under the Code's definition of "sexual offense." If the uncharged act does not qualify, then it is not admissible against you under this rule.

---

[135] Deskbook, CH. 15.

The Takeaway

MRE 413 is an exception to the general rule that evidence of other crimes cannot be introduced at trial. This exception applies only to sexual assault cases, and only in instances where the previous crime was also sexual assault. To introduce it at trial, the prosecution must convince the judge that the prior charge is relevant to the present case.

To block the admission of evidence of the prior offense, your attorney must show either that you were not given proper notice of the prosecution's intent to use it, or that the prior offense does not meet the military's definition of sexual assault.

The Trial Process

Panel Selection

Chapter 10

Chapters 7–9 cover the trial itself. After the motions hearing, the next step is the selection of the panel that will act as jury in your trial. The defense and prosecution attorneys question potential panelists and select those they believe most able to hear your case fairly and with an open mind. A good attorney will also use this process to establish credibility and rapport with the panel.

Once motions are finished, your next appearance will very likely be the trial. The big day. Typically, the first substantive portion of your trial will be panel selection. This is the process where your attorney and the military prosecutor pick the service members who will be on the panel. The convening authority selects the panel pool. Typically, anywhere from 12-20 potential panel members will arrive in their dress uniform at the courthouse on the first day of trial. After preliminary matters are discussed, the military judge will call in these potential panel members, and they will sit in the jury box. From there, the voir dire process of selecting the panel begins.

First, the military judge will ask the potential panel members a series of questions followed by the military prosecutor and your defense attorney. The potential panel members will first be asked questions as a group. After that, there will be individual voir dire where the judge and attorneys can probe deeper into answers provided by a panel member.

Your attorney's job during voir dire is to select a panel that is open-minded, understanding, receptive to your theory of the case, and ultimately fair. This is your attorney's first interaction with the people that will be deciding your fate. He should be empathetic and patient, and he should be doing everything he can from this early stage to earn the trust of the panel. In trial, credibility is king.

Your attorney should be focusing on presenting himself in a positive light before the panel. He should be confident, comfortable, and, most importantly, respectful. The potential panel members will be watching his every move. This is especially true of civilian defense attorneys. I think, based on experience, that panel members are hesitant to like and trust an outsider. This can be overcome quickly if your attorney is likable, humble, and easy to talk to. Your attorney also needs to be focused on learning the beliefs and attitudes of these potential jurors to make sure that none of them possess inherent bias against you or your position. Finally, if the military judge allows, voir dire is an opportunity to gauge who in the panel pool is open to your theory of defense.

Before the start of the trial, your attorneys will be given panel questionnaires. These packets contain basic questions about the jurors such as their age, name, rank, education level, service record, marital and family history, hobbies, and other basic background questions. Your attorneys must be familiar with each potential juror and review these packets thoroughly before trial. Understanding a panel member's background, service history, and experiences in life are the most useful predictors when trying to figure out whether that panel member will be open to your theory of the case.

The military judge will start the questioning with the potential panel members to determine whether there is a basis to excuse the member from the trial. The judge will ask questions to make sure that each panel member can follow the law and disregard any training the panel member has had on sexual assault. The military judge will ask a series of questions on the burden of proof to make sure that each panel member understands that you are presumed innocent and that the burden of proof remains with the government at all times.

Once the military judge is finished, counsel will ask the panel members as a group a series of questions. How your attorney asks these questions and the atmosphere your attorney creates is very, very important. I typically start my questioning by disclosing something personal about myself to create an environment where panel members feel comfortable. From there, I ask short, nonleading, open-ended questions, and I ask these questions in a warm and friendly manner. I will leave the podium, stand in front of the prospective panel members, make eye contact, and simply talk with these individuals. I stand without notes, and I concentrate on building rapport with each person in front of me. My entire goal is to create an atmosphere where the potential panel members are comfortable sharing important details with me that will allow me to decide if they will give you, my client, a fair trial.

Your attorneys, the military judge, and government counsel will all be recording who answers what to each question. After group voir dire is over, the military judge will ask both parties which people they would like to question individually. This all depends on how the potential panel member answered the question. For example, if a panel member has a person in their lives that was the victim of sexual assault, I am going to want to question that person in individual voir dire to determine whether that person can be fair and open-minded and put aside their personal experiences in deciding your case.

Following individual voir dire, the military judge will ask both sides whether there are any jurors that counsel wish to be removed for cause. Removal for cause means that based on their answers to questions, the attorneys do not feel that the individual can put aside their personal experiences or beliefs and be fair. Military courts recognize a difference between implied bias and actual bias.[136] Actual bias is focused on whether the panel member who is being challenged for cause cannot move from their belief or opinion. For example, I have had some panel members simply believe that the accused should testify if he is truly an innocent person. I would certainly request that this panel member be removed for actual bias. Implied bias assumes that if the potential member were to serve, "the system's appearance of fairness is necessarily implicated."[137]

Each side in a military sexual assault trial is entitled to an unlimited number of challenges for cause.[138] These challenges will be litigated before the military judge and counsel will argue for or against the potential panel member staying on the case. The law states that challenges for cause should be granted liberally.[139] This means that the military judge should grant your attorney's request to remove a potential panel member as long as the challenge is not speculative or clearly without merit.[140] It is also important to remember that challenges for cause can be made at any point during the trial.[141]

Your attorneys are also entitled to one peremptory challenge. A peremptory challenge results in the exclusion of a potential juror without the need for any reason or explanation—unless the opposing party presents a prima facie argument that this challenge

---

[136] Military Criminal Justice, Practice and Procedure, Eighth Edition, Ch 15-10(C), David A Schlueter.
[137] Id.
[138] Id.
[139] United States v. White, 35 M.J. 284 (C.M.A. 1993).
[140] United States v. Keenan, 39 M.J. 150 (A.C.M.R. 1994).
[141] Military Criminal Justice, Practice and Procedure, Eighth Edition, Ch 15-10(D), David A Schlueter.

was used to discriminate based on race, ethnicity, or sex.[142] If your attorney argues that the only reason the military prosecutor used his peremptory challenge was the juror's race or sex, the military charge judge must then determine whether the military prosecutor provided a neutral reason with a clear and specific reason for their peremptory challenge against that panelist. If the military prosecutor can do that, the military judge will grant their request.

Voir dire is one of the most important moments in the trial. These panelists hold your future in their hands. Remember, most panelists are apprehensive and intimidated by the court-martial process. Officers and senior enlisted members are especially worried that their ignorance about how the system works will be exposed. Your attorney's job is to turn that around. Your attorney should change the panel members from being strangers to friends. In short, the voir dire process is your attorney's opportunity to win over the panelists and show those members that he can be trusted.

The Takeaway

Panel selection is the first step in the trial. It takes place through voir dire, which is the process of questioning potential panelists to determine which ones seem capable of hearing your case with an open mind and assessing it fairly.

These are the steps in the voir dire process:

- The panelists fill out written questionnaires with information about their backgrounds.
- The judge questions the panelists as a group to make sure they all understand the basic criteria for acting as a juror, including the presumption that you are innocent and that the prosecution's job is to prove otherwise.
- The attorneys take turns questioning the panelists, first as a group and then individually.

---

[142] Batson v. Kentucky, 476 U.S. 79 (1986); see also United States v. Santiago-Davila, 26 M.J. 380 (C.M.A.)

Panel Selection

- If necessary, the attorneys challenge each other on the choice of specific panelists either for cause or peremptorily.

Voir dire is the first time your attorney interacts with the panel. A good attorney will use this opportunity to establish trust and rapport with the panelists.

Opening Statements: Tell Your Story

Chapter 11

A trial begins with both sides making their opening statements. Your attorney has established credibility and rapport with the panelist during voir dire; the opening statement can build on that by telling your story in vivid language that makes them "see" the events in question. A compelling opening statement introduces your attorney's theory and themes in the case, addresses its weaknesses, and informs the panelists that you want them to find in your favor.

Popular culture reveres the closing argument. Movies like *My Cousin Vinny* or *A Time to Kill* emphasize the importance of the closing statement. Who can forget, "now imagine she's white"? The entire courtroom stops; the judge is touched by emotion, and the jury is in tears. In reality, however, study after study has shown that jury verdicts are far more consistent with their first impressions than their last. In other words, most panel members make up their minds in just a few minutes whether to trust your attorney, like you, and ultimately root for you. The only thing your attorney must sell to the panel is his credibility. That trust is introduced during voir dire and developed during the opening statement. Win your opening statement, and you will likely win your case.

Great opening statements, like great trial work, are based on storytelling. As humans, we are genetically designed to love a good story. Before our ancestors could speak, farm, or even walk fully upright, they told stories. They drew pictures on walls and designs in the dirt, and transferred their culture from generation to generation by storytelling. Religion is based on storytelling. Literature is based on storytelling. Movies are based on storytelling. You can be the top attorney in your Harvard class, but if you cannot tell a good story, you cannot be a great trial attorney.

You and your attorney must develop your story. The story must be simple, easy to understand, and rooted in common sense. Is it more likely that you raped her while she slept or that she invited you into her room and did not want to tell her husband the truth? Is it more likely that you ripped her clothes off by force or with her consent? Is it more likely that you are a predator or just a college kid who had drunken sex with the wrong person? The opening statement is about telling your story.

Introduction. Typically, I have already introduced myself during voir dire. So, I usually will not stand up there and say, "Good morning, my name is Robert Capovilla." My partner will not say, "Hello, my name is Mickey Williams." During the first few seconds in opening statements, I want to build upon the trust I developed in voir dire. I want the panel to feel comfortable with me. One way to make that happen is to admit something personal about myself or show humility. I do not want that panel to think I am some outsider in an expensive suit who is paid to say whatever my client wants. So, usually, I start my opening off with something like this:

"I know that voir dire can be an uncomfortable experience. I certainly hope that no one was offended by my questions. I am sorry if I offended anyone. In fact, as I stand here right now, I am nervous myself. I am afraid that I will not say the right things or that I will forget something important. I am afraid that my mistakes will hurt my client. Ladies and gentlemen, as this case unfolds, I will most certainly make mistakes. I may do things that you do not like. I am far from perfect. I ask that when I make those mistakes you hold me responsible and not my client."

This kind of introduction builds trust with the panel. I strip myself of any conceit or arrogance and allow the panel to see me as a person. Besides, some degree of self-deprecation typically will endear me to the panel. They will relax and realize that they are not the only ones afraid to appear nervous or scared. In other words, I build trust with them and credibility.

What is Your Theory of Defense? After introductions, I will want to introduce my theory of the case. A theory is your side of the case, and it is your side of what happened. Your attorney's theory of the case must be logical, organized, and simple to understand. Typically, I talk about my theme or themes within the first minute of the opening statement. You should have no more than 3-4 themes in your case.

What is Your Theme? I am not a big proponent of the two- or three-word catchy themes during trials. I often find that such themes are forced, unnatural, and cheapen your defense. I do, however, like two or three themes to help explain my theory of defense. Themes should summarize your attorney's position in the case, they should be engaging but not cheap, and they should be easy to remember. Themes are the anchors that you build your case around. As a society, we love themes. They help us understand stories, and they are memorable. Great movies and books have wonderful themes. The original *Rocky* had an incredible theme: "his whole life was a million to one shot." This theme is easy to understand. We remember it. Most importantly, it fits with the facts.

I will usually introduce my theme before I list my theories. A typical opening statement may sound something like this:

Theme: "Ladies and gentlemen, this is a case about an accuser who will do whatever she can to save her marriage, career, and reputation." Theories: "In fact, as this case unfolds, you will find out that the following three facts are true:

1. First. PFC Jane was married when she sent my client nude pictures. She was married when she sent my client a text message at 2300 to come to her house. She was married when she had sex with my client. She did not report this alleged assault until her husband found her phone. And now she is doing everything she can to save her marriage.
2. Second. You will find out in this case that minutes before PFC Jane met with CID, she deleted all of the text messages she sent to my client. She deleted all of the Facebook messages she sent to my client. And she deleted all the pictures that she sent to my client. PFC Jane destroyed evidence in this case.
3. Third. The government will not be able to present a single eyewitness to corroborate PFC Jane's case. There were 15 other airmen at the party when my client allegedly assaulted PFC Jane. In fact, they were standing right outside the bedroom door. Not one of them heard an assault, saw an assault, or suspected an assault. In fact, the defense will call two of those witnesses during our case. These witnesses will tell you that moments after allegedly being assaulted, PFC Jane played beer pong, danced with our client, and appeared to be having a wonderful time."

Storytelling. Once I introduce myself, my theme, and my theories of defense, I will tell the story of my case. Remember, credibility is king during trial, so the facts must support the story. If I can, I tell the story based only on the evidence that I know I can elicit during cross-examination. If I have a few solid witnesses to testify during my case, I will base the story on what they will testify to. However, I must be very careful not to oversell our story or state facts that cannot be justified during the trial. Otherwise, I risk losing the panel's trust. Once that happens, I am done.

When I tell the story of your case, I focus on the people, the places, and the atmosphere. I do not focus on the law. The judge will instruct the panel on the law; my job is to emphasize the events, not the legalities of the case. A great story is a simple story, it makes sense, and is not too long. A simple story is a story that is credible, believable, and aligns with the panel's notions of common sense. We love movies like *Gladiator* or *Braveheart* because they align with our notions of justice and fair play.

The story must be told in a vivid manner that recreates for the jury the events in question. I always use an active voice when I give an opening statement. I want the jury to feel the story with me. To be clear, I am not promoting over-the-top opening statements where I yell or cry or get emotional. I am promoting strong, detailed storytelling. I want the jury to relive the moment when the accuser invites my client into her bedroom. Finally, good storytelling must be organized storytelling. Typically, this means I follow a chronological order. Panel members are used to hearing stories from beginning to end. Such a story is easy to understand and to tell. Do not complicate matters.

Request a Not Guilty. I never finish an opening statement without telling the panel exactly what I want. I tell the panel what a favorable outcome in the case is for my client. I try to be conversational with the panel during the entire trial as much as possible. I typically do not say, "at the conclusion of these proceedings, I will ask you to acquit my client of all charges and specifications." Typically, I say something like this: "Ladies and gentlemen, my client has been under investigation for two years, and the evidence will show that he has been falsely accused. At the conclusion of this trial, I'm going to simply ask you to let my client finally go home." Remember, these panel members, even if they are 0-5 or 0-6 officers, are not attorneys. Your lawyer should strive to be as professional and conversational as possible.

Do Not Oversell Your Case. I must reemphasize this because it is that important—your attorney should not oversell the case in the opening. The only thing your attorney must sell to the jury is credibility. Once that is gone, you cannot get it back. There is nothing more damaging to an opening statement than making promises you cannot keep. The panel will remember it, the government will call you out on it, and your attorney will look silly. When in doubt, exercise caution in the opening statement and do not risk losing the only thing you have to give.

Confront Weaknesses. When you and your attorney know that there are weaknesses in the case and you know those weaknesses are admissible at trial, be open and honest in the opening statement about them. Do not try to hide these weaknesses or pretend they do not exist. Tell the panel about the weakness, use the evidence at your disposal to minimize it, and do not ignore it. Credibility is about being honest with the panel, which includes disclosing favorable and unfavorable facts. The last thing that you want is for your attorney to look like she is hiding evidence. It is all about credibility.

No Argument in Opening Statements. I explain to my clients that the opening statement is about the story, the people, the themes, and the atmosphere. The opening statement is not an argument. I cannot stand up during opening and say that your accuser is a liar. I can, however, point out all the times that she changed her story. The opening statement is about stating facts and weaving those facts into a common-sense-driven story. The closing statement is where your attorney will argue the facts. Your attorney needs to be mindful of the judge here as well. Some judges will allow a bit of argument, and others will not. Know the judge. Objections made during the opening statement can throw your attorney off and break his rhythm. Do not argue in the opening statements.

The Takeaway

Panelists' first impressions during a trial tend to shape their conclusions at the end of it. It is critical that your attorney's opening statement build on the credibility established during voir dire to tell your story in a compelling, believable way. The opening statement is not the place to instruct the panel about matters of law, or to argue the prosecution's claims.

An effective opening statement:

- Puts the panelists into your story by vividly evoking the people, places, and atmosphere of the incident in question, and keeps the narrative simple, chronological, and rooted in common sense.
- Introduces your attorney's theory of defense and its themes. The themes are the essential ideas you want the panelists to keep in mind as they listen to arguments. They should be simply stated, engaging, and easy for the panelists to remember.
- Informs the panel what the defense team is looking for from them: a not-guilty verdict.
- Confronts the weaknesses in your case head-on, and is careful not to oversell your case by making claims that can't be supported with evidence later on.

Direct Examination: In Another's Eyes

Chapter 12

Direct examination is where the attorneys call their own witnesses to the stand and question them. The objective in direct examination is to prompt your witness to tell your story for you, in his or her own words. The witness should use language that allows the panelists to relive the events in question, and your attorney should ask open-ended questions that allow the witness to tell the story their own way.

After the prosecution rests its case-in-chief (the main evidence and arguments in its case), it will be your turn to present evidence, call witnesses, and maybe even testify. There are also times where the defense does not present any evidence or call any witnesses. This happens if you and your attorney feel like you have the case in the bag and cannot present more helpful information. I have won several jury trials where I did not put on a case-in-chief at all. Remember, as the accused, you do not have to present any evidence. The burden is on the government to prove your case beyond a reasonable doubt. It is always nice to call witnesses or present evidence that supports your theory of the case, and I will call those types of witnesses if the benefit is high and the risk low.

Unlike cross-examination or opening statements, a great direct examination is one where the witness and his story are the center of attention, not the lawyer. Direct examination is about telling your story through the lens of another person in a forceful, clear, and efficient way. Like any well-written story, a good direct examination should bring the panel to the place and time of the actual events. The direct examination should be told in the active voice, and it should allow the panel to relive the events from the perspective of the accused.

There are a few rules that I live by when conducting direct examinations or preparing a witness for direct examination. First, I want to keep the direct examination and my questions simple. I want my questions to be easy to understand and easy to follow. Remember, by the time trial rolls around, you and your attorney know your case frontwards and backward. You know what every witness will testify to, and you know whether the information will be helpful or harmful. Panels, on the other hand, have no prior information about your case beside what they have learned sitting and listening. Therefore, it is very important to keep the questions simple and easy to understand. This way, the panel can follow along without getting confused.

Most people only have attention spans that last 15-20 minutes. Just like in the opening statements, your attorney should not be long-winded. Your attorney needs to know what important facts the witness can present, get to those facts quickly, develop those facts, and then move on. There is nothing more frustrating to a panel than listening to a witness drone on and on about trivial matters. Get to the point. Hit it hard. Move on.

I also like to organize my direct examinations in chronological order. Again, these jurors do not know the facts of your case, they do not know these witnesses, and they are doing their best to understand. As people, we react to stories best when those stories are in chronological order. When conducting a direct examination, I will start with the witness's background information, ask the witness to describe the scene and the action, and then do my best to highlight the main points of the witness's testimony. Stay in order; present the evidence in simple form; and follow a chronological timeline. This will allow the panel to keep up and fully understand the benefit of the witnesses' testimony. If your attorney is jumping around from scene to scene and person to person, the panel will simply stop listening. Keep it simple. Keep it organized. Keep it chronological.

I also use transition statements to help the witness stay organized and the panel focused. Again, panel members do not know why your attorney has called the witness, and they do not know why the witness is important. Good transition statements will help the panel understand the importance of the witnesses' testimony. Here is an example I have used in the past:

> Q: SSG White, I now want to turn your attention to the party that took place in your hotel room after dinner. What time did the party start? Who was in attendance? When did the party end?

The transition statement allows the panel to follow my lead. I may not be telling the story, but I act as the conductor, and I want to make sure my passengers are with me. These kinds of transitions help the panel stay focused, attentive, and clear. Before describing what happened at a scene, I first want the witness to describe the scene. This provides context and understanding to the panel member who needs it. Before asking the important questions, set the stage. Who was at the party? Lights on or off? Drinking? How many people were there? These questions place the panel at the party. Then, I ask the substantive questions:

> Q: Did you see my client at the party?
> A: Yes.

Direct Examination: In Another's Eyes

Q: Where was my client when you first saw him?
A: He was sitting next to PFC Moon ([the accuser]).
Q: Where were they sitting?
A: Both of them were on the bed. Sitting next to each other.
Q: What was my client wearing?
A: Shorts and a t-shirt.
Q: What was PFC Moon wearing?
A: She was wearing shorts and a white tank top.
Q: Were the lights off or on when you saw my client sitting next to PFC Moon?
A: They were on. I could see them really well. They were talking to each other.
Q: How far away were you from my client and PFC Moon when you saw them talking?
A: Oh…maybe 3-4 feet. I could hear them clearly. That's for sure.
Q: Were you sitting in a chair or standing when you saw them on the bed together?
A: I was standing near the bathroom door.
Q: Was there music playing at the party?
A: Yes. But it was not loud. Besides, I saw them sitting together early at the party before most of the people got there.
Q: Could you hear what PFC Moon and SGT White were talking about?
A: Yes. Clearly.
Q: How much distance was there between my client and PFC Moon on the bed?
A: None. They were sitting shoulder to shoulder. Very close to each other.
Q: What did PFC Moon say to my client while they were sitting there talking?
A: She said she wanted to leave the hotel with him. She said she wanted to show him her room.

Q: Based on your personal observations of PFC Moon at the time, was she smiling when she said this to my client?
A: Oh yes. She was laughing and giggling.
Q: Did she touch my client when she asked him to leave the hotel room with her?
A: She put her hand on his lap. I saw that.
Q: Where was she looking when she put her hand on my client's lap?
A: Right at SGT White. She was smiling, like I said.
Q: What did SGT White do when she asked him to leave the party?
A: He told her he was worried that her husband might find out. He didn't want them to get in trouble.
Q: Did PFC Moon say anything in response?
A: She told SGT White not to worry about it. She said it would be their secret.
Q: Tell me what happened after PFC Moon said that to SGT White?
A: They both got up and left the party together.

Those questions are clear, simple, and easy to follow. I get right to the point. Notice, I do not ask the witness if PFC Moon was flirting with my client; instead, I have him describe the flirtation to the panel. I allow the witness to paint a picture for the panel that they understand and can follow. I will argue in closing that this was a flirtation. As Ernest Hemingway said, great stories are shown and not told. The panel will walk away from this line of questioning and know everything that I want them to know.

Present Tense. I always want to ask my questions in the present tense, and I want the witness to answer the questions in the present tense. Remember, my goal is to recreate what the witness saw for the panel. I cannot do this if I am constantly asking questions in the past tense. I want the panel to feel like they are in that hotel room. I want them to see my client on that bed, sitting there, and

I want them to see the accuser flirting with him. This is good storytelling. And good storytelling wins the day.

Nonleading Questions. For the most part, the military rules of evidence do not let me use leading questions during direct examination. A leading question is a question that suggests the answer to the witness. During direct examination, I must ask open-ended questions that do not suggest an answer to the witness.

> Leading Question: PFC White jumped in the hot tub naked, right?
> Open-Ended: At any point did PFC White swim in the hot tub?

Open-ended questions allow the witness to tell their story without undue influence from the attorney. A lot of inexperienced attorneys will try to lead witnesses during direct examination. This is a mistake. First, it will draw an objection that the military judge will sustain. But second, it detracts from the witness's credibility. Remember, direct examination is about letting the witness tell the story in their own words. Cross-examination questions do not allow the witness to do that. The attorney should not do anything during direct examination that will diminish her witness's credibility in the panel's eyes.

Position of the Witness. During direct examination, I want the witness engaged with the panel in an authentic and credible manner. When directing a witness, I usually move the podium closer to the panel so that when the witness speaks, the witness can look directly at the panel. This allows the witness to actively engage the panel and look them in the eyes. I do not want my witness to appear coached, but I do want my witness actively looking at the panel when answering questions. Again, direct examination is about the credibility of the witness, not the attorney. The witness should be prepared, confident, and credible. Good attorneys will interview a witness as many times as it takes before trial to make sure the witness and the attorney have a good rapport. Your attorney should never, ever put a witness on the stand before speaking to them. That is a cardinal trial sin.

The Takeaway

Direct examination is about telling your story through your witness. Your attorney should be the conductor, eliciting a narrative from the witness that is authentically theirs. The attorney only facilitates the testimony and is never the center of attention. Good direct examination:

- Keeps the language in the present tense, allowing the panel to relive the events in question.
- Asks short, simple questions designed to address the events in question in chronological order.
- Asks open-ended, non-leading questions. Allowing the witness to produce his or her own testimony adds to the witness' credibility.
- Physically positions the witness so that he or she is able to make direct eye contact with the panelists.

Cross-Examination: Win Your Story

Chapter 13

The cross-examination of the government's witnesses is probably the best tool your attorney can use in your defense. It can expose contradictions and false claims for what they are, and reveal the truth. Successful cross-examination requires good preparation, self-restraint, and flexibility.

The trial is about finding out the truth. And there is no better way to expose the truth than to cross-examine your accuser effectively during the trial. Sexual assault cases are won during opening statements and cross-examination of the accuser. Win the opening. Win the cross. Go home. I love cross-examination.

Cross-examination is misunderstood. Popular culture and inexperienced trial attorneys believe that cross-examination should result in the witness standing up and saying, "Ok…you win. I am a liar. I am a dirty, dirty liar. Please leave me alone now." Very rarely does cross-examination take such a dramatic turn. Instead, cross-examination is another way for you and your attorney to tell your story. Except, during cross-examination, your attorney will be telling your story through the government's witnesses. As legendary trial attorney Gerry Spence writes, "Basic cross-examination is nothing more than a true-or-false test administered to the witness, in the course of which our story, as it concerns that witness, is told."[143]

You and your attorney must know what your theory of defense is. Once you know your theory, you can tell your story truly and honestly. Cross-examination is another tool to tell that honest story. Young attorneys think that cross-examination is all about the witnesses' answers. They only ask questions that they know will be answered in their favor by the witness. I do not care what the witness says to me on the stand. I care about telling our story to the panel. Then it will be up to the panel to decide who is telling the truth.

Here is an example. Last year I had a trial where the accuser claimed that my client sexually assaulted her in a hotel room. She testified on direct examination that my client grabbed her by her wrists and forced her inside his hotel room. Once inside the room, she alleged that my client grabbed the back of her neck and ripped her pants off. He held her down and sexually assaulted her. She fought back the entire time and even alleged to have scratched him and hit him. She did not report this alleged assault until her husband heard a rumor that she slept with my client while she was on temporary duty assignment. This was five months later. Here is a sample of my cross:

> Q: You and my client walked hand in hand to his hotel room, right?
> A: No. He grabbed me.
> Q: My client opened the door to his hotel room, right?
> A: Yes.
> Q: He walked in first?
> A: I don't remember.

---

[143] <u>Win Your Case</u>, Exposing the Hidden Truth – Cross-examination. Gerry Spence.

Q: You walked in right behind him?
A: I don't remember. He forced me in. Grabbed me really hard.
Q: You walked to the bed?
A: You mean after he grabbed me?! [Note: We never answer questions, we ask them.]
Q: You got on top of the bed?
A: He made me.
Q: You told my client it was ok?
A: I never said that.
Q: You told my client it would be your secret?
A: No. That's what he said.
Q: You and my client kissed one another?
A: It didn't happen like that.
Q: You stood up and took your pants off?
A: He forced me.
Q: You told my client to take his pants off?
A: I would never do that.
Q: You performed oral sex on my client?
A: No. Never. Gross.
Q: You and my client engaged in intercourse in that hotel?
A: If you mean he raped me, then yes.
Q: When the sex was over, you put your pants back on?
A: I don't remember how my pants got back on.
Q: My client stayed in the bed?
A: I did not pay attention to him.
Q: You walked to the door?
A: Yes. To leave.
Q: You opened the door?
A: Yes. To leave.
Q: You looked outside in the hallway?
A: Yes. I was embarrassed. I did not want anyone to get the wrong idea.

Q: You wanted to make sure nobody was in the hall?
A: Yes.
Q: You looked at my client and said, remember our secret?
A: I don't remember.
Q: You left the hotel room?
A: Yes.

In the above instance, I do not care what the witness says. I am getting my story of the case out there. It makes almost no difference to me what her answers are. I am telling my story to the panel. The government's next witness was a member of the accuser's unit who was with her on TDY. Here is a sample of my cross.

Q: You saw A1C Wright [the accuser] leave the party?
A: Yes. I saw them both leave.
Q: She left the party with my client?
A: Yes. They left together.
Q: You watched the two of them leave together?
A: Yes.
Q: Once you saw them leave, you opened the door to the hallway?
A: Yes. I was concerned they might do something stupid.
Q: You watched them walk down the hallway together?
A: Yes.
Q: They were holding hands?
A: Yes.
Q: My client did not force her to hold his hand?
A: Not that I saw. They were just holding hands normal.
Q: She did not pull away when my client held her hand?
A: Not that I saw.

Q: That was the last time you saw A1C Wright that night?
A: Yes.
Q: You saw A1C Wright the next morning?
A: Yes.
Q: You saw her around 0830?
A: Yes.
Q: You two had breakfast together?
A: We did.
Q: You two ate breakfast in the lobby of the hotel?
A: Yes.
Q: You sat right across from her during breakfast?
A: Yes. She was right in front of me. We ate together.
Q: There was maybe two feet separating her from you?
A: Two or three feet. Yes.
Q: The lights were on in the hotel during the breakfast?
A: Yes.
Q: You could see A1C Wright's face clearly?
A: Yes.
Q: You did not see any scratches on her face? [A1C Wright testified that my client grabbed her face and forced her to kiss him.]
A: I did not.
Q: You did not see any bruises on her face?
A: I did not.
Q: You did not see any red marks on her face?
A: No. Her face looks like it always does.
Q: You could see A1C Wright's neck, right? [A1C Wright testified that my client grabbed her by the neck and threw her on the bed.]
A: Yes.
Q: No scratches?
Q: No bruises?

Q: No red marks?
Q: You spoke to A1C Wright?
A: Yes.
Q: You asked her what happened with my client the night before?
A: I asked her if she needed to talk about anything, yes.
Q: She told you nothing happened?
A: She said he just walked her back to her room, yes.
Q: She told you that my client walked her back to her room?
A: Yes. That's what she said.
Q: You told her she needed to be careful?
A: Yes.
Q: You told her that she could get in trouble for cheating on her husband?
A: Yes. We all know that. The Air Force takes that stuff seriously.

During this cross-examination, I am using the government's witness to cast doubt on the accuser's story. This is gold. Now, I do not have to call my client to the stand and ask him whether he put his hands on the accuser's throat. I do not have to ask him if he grabbed her face. I have everything I need, through the government's witness, to argue during closing that the accuser's story is called into question by the government's own witness. Moreover, this witness also provides me information to challenge the entire premise that the accuser was ever in my client's room. Cross-examination is the best tool a defense attorney can use to expose the truth.

The Rules of Cross-Examination

Cross-examination is an art, not a science. However, there are certain rules that should almost always be followed:

1. *Keep it Brief.* Every question asked must be asked with a purpose. That purpose should be to support your theme or theory of the case or impeach your accuser's credibility. Attorneys should never just rehash what your accuser said on direct examination. The panel will tune your attorney out and stop listening. Cross-examination is about telling your story and giving your attorney ammunition for the closing argument. If the question is not relevant to those points, dump it.
2. *Primacy and Recency.* Your attorney should ask his most powerful questions at the start and the conclusion of the examination. Typically, if your accuser changed her story during direct examination, I would hit them with those changes in their story first. This establishes up front that the witness cannot be trusted. I love to open with a bang. The panel's first impression and last impressions will stay with them. Start strong and finish strong.
3. *Do Not Rehash Direct Examination.* I see this all the time. The accuser testifies on direct. The defense attorney is not experienced and asks fifty questions that did not need to be touched on again. Cross is about your story. Your attorney needs to hit your theories and themes, attack your accuser's credibility, and then sit down. There is no need to cover every topic covered by the government again.
4. *Know the Answers to Your Questions.* Cross-examination is not discovery. Your attorney should not use cross-examination as a tool to find out what really happened. By the time your accuser takes the stand, your attorney should know everything that she is going to say. On cross-examination, your attorney should know the answer to every question he asks. Mind you, this does not mean we care about the

answers, but it does mean we know what the witness is going to say. There is nothing more humiliating than being unprepared for cross-examination.

5. *Listen to the Answers.* I see a lot of attorneys bury their noses in their notes during cross-examination. It is as though no matter what your accuser says, they are going to ask the next question that they have written out. These types of attorneys are afraid to look silly, and they lack confidence. Your attorney must have the ability to listen and then adjust on the fly. Your attorney must be flexible. Witnesses change their stories all the time. The best moments I have had in a courtroom are unscripted. Listen. Listen. Listen. Sometimes your accuser will give you pearls, and your attorney will need to be ready to take advantage.

6. *Do Not Argue with the Witness.* I have done this. Every attorney alive has done this. As soon as the witness says something your attorney does not like, an argument breaks out. This cannot ever happen. Your attorney must remain calm, cool, and collected. First, arguing with a witness is not allowed and can really annoy the judge. Second, arguing with a witness will almost certainly hurt your attorney's credibility before the panel. Remember, credibility is king. Your attorney should be a professional, and professionals do not ever argue with the witness.

7. *Never Ask the Witness to Explain.* Cross-examination is about witness control and asking short, closed-ended questions. Your attorney should not be asking the witness open-ended questions, and he should not be asking a witness to explain. The witness will have the opportunity to explain during the redirect examination. Until then, tell your story and let the prosecutor try to clean it up.

8. *Be Organized.* A great cross-examination is not just about courtroom performance; it is about preparation before trial. My cross-examinations mirror my themes and theories. I use each theme and theory as a roadmap or chapter to effectively cross-examine the accuser.

Cross-examination Organization. When it comes to organizing my cross-examination of the accuser, I take each theme and break it down into chapters. Below is a good example of how I organize my cross-examinations. Here, the theme of my case was that the accuser lied about having sex with my client to save her marriage and that she did not report the alleged sexual assault until she found out that my client was telling people in the unit that they had sex. The accuser's husband was stationed on the same base as my client and the accuser.

In this case, the accuser was caught having an affair about three months before she had sex with my client. When her husband found out about this previous affair, he beat the hell out of the accuser's boyfriend and told the accuser that if she cheated again, he would divorce her. After the fight, the accuser and her husband were working things out. This meant that if her husband found out about my client, the accuser's marriage would be over, and the trust would be gone forever.

In the chart below, I have three columns: question, citation, and relevance. I want to know the source of every question that I ask. This way, if the accuser changes her story, I can impeach her credibility on the spot and know exactly who to call if she denies that specific fact. The relevance section reminds me exactly why I am asking the question. This helps me stay focused, to the point, and in control.

I first put a title for my overall theme. Here, that title is, "I MUST Preserve My Marriage." The title keeps me organized and focused. Next, I write a little blurb about the accuser's mindset. This again reminds me of what I want to accomplish. Then, I start

Chapter I. Underneath the chapter title, I again have a little blurb designed to keep me focused and exacting. The letters Id. simply mean that the citation is the same cite as quoted above.

I MUST Preserve My Marriage

When my husband found out that I was texting inappropriate messages to SSgt Boyfriend, he wanted to knock his teeth in. It caused problems in my marriage. The last thing I want to do is admit to him that I hooked up with SSgt Accused.

Chapter I
I Met SSgt. Boyfriend, We Exchanged Sexual Text Messages, and I Lied Under Oath about that Relationship.

Question	Citation	Relevance
You married SrA Sucker in 2017?	21 Nov 19 Interview With Accuser.	Developing the marriage. Background information.
After you got married, you joined the Air Force?	Id.	Id.
He joined the Air Force 6 months after you did?	Id.	Id.
You arrived at Big Foot AFB in March or April 2017, right?	Id.	Id.
You were married to SrA Sucker when you arrived at Big Foot AFB?	Id.	Establishing that the accuser was married when she arrived on base.

SrA Sucker was stationed with you at Big Foot AFB?	Id.	Establishing that accuser's husband was stationed at the same base as accuser and my client.
You two were stationed at Big Foot AFB together?	Id.	Id.
You first met SSgt Boyfriend in the spring of 2017?	SSgt Boyfriend Prior Motions Testimony from 25 November 19.	Establishing foundation for relationship with SSgt Boyfriend.
SSgt Boyfriend was a law enforcement officer like you?		Establishing that SSgt Boyfriend knew they could get in trouble for inappropriate relationship.
SSgt Boyfriend was also stationed at Big Foot AFB?	Id.	Laying foundation for inappropriate relationship.
You two worked in the same squadron?		
SSgt Boyfriend was married when you met him?		
His wife was pregnant when the two of you met?	Id.	Developing relationship. Laying foundation for inappropriate relationship.
By the Spring of 2018, you started to text SSgt Boyfriend about things going		

111

on in your life, right?	
He started to text you about things going on in his personal life, right?	
In fact, you confided in him about your mother being sick?	
He confided in you about his father being sick?	
At times, he called your cell phone several times a week?	
Sometimes even several times a day?	
Over time, your relationship with SSgt Boyfriend grew and he started sending you text messages like, "I really want you," right?	SSgt Boyfriend's Phone

You would respond to those sexual text messages with messages of your own that read, "I really want you too," right?	SSgt Lopez, SSgt Boyfriend Prior Motions Testimony from 25 November 19.	
You sent him text messages stating things like, "I really want to please you?"	Id.	Laying foundation for inappropriate relationship. If accuser denies, impeach with SSgt Boyfriend's testimony.
On 25 November 2019, you testified at a hearing before this military judge in this very courtroom?	Accuser's Motions Testimony from 25 November 19.	Laying foundation that accuser lied under oath and committed perjury, which is a crime of dishonesty.

That hearing was about your relationship with SSgt Boyfriend? You were placed under oath? You swore to tell the truth? Major Military Prosecutor was in the courtroom? Captain Military Prosecutor was in the courtroom? Your SVC was in the courtroom? During this hearing I asked you several questions about your relationship with SSgt Boyfriend?	Id.	Building up the suspense to properly impeach the accuser in front of the panel.
You're a law enforcement officer?	Accuser's Service Record	She understands the law.
You understood that you have a legal duty to tell the truth when placed under oath?	Id.	Id.

As a law enforcement officer, you understand that if you lie under oath, you are committing a crime?	Id.	Id.
That crime is called perjury, right?	Id.	Id.
At that hearing, I asked you the following question: "at any point in the spring of 2018 was your relationship with SSgt Boyfriend otherwise inappropriate for a married woman?"	Accuser's Motions Testimony from 25 November 19. DC – And those text messages were not romantic in nature according to "undetectable" is that correct? NP – Yes sir DC – They were about your father. Correct? NP – Yes sir	Confronting the accuser with her prior statements.
You answered that question by stating: No, sir.	Accuser's Motions Testimony from 25 November 19.	Admissible under MRE 801. Prior inconsistent statement made under oath.
I'm going to ask you again, now, while you're still under oath, you sent SSgt Boyfriend sexual	SSgt Boyfriend's Motions Testimony from 25 November 19.	Showing the panel that this witness has no problem lying to get what she wants. Even if

text messages that were inappropriate for a married woman to send, right?		that means breaking the law.
So, you lied under oath in a hearing before this military judge?	Id.	Id.
At that same hearing on 25 November 2019, I asked you if you ever texted SSgt Boyfriend in a sexual manner, right? I asked you if you ever sent him a text message that read: "I want you?" I want to please you?	Accuser's Motions Testimony from 25 November 19. DC – And those text messages were not romantic in nature according to "undetectable" is that correct? NP – Yes sir DC – They were about your father, correct? NP – Yes sir	Again, confronting the witness with her prior inconsistent statements. Panel needs to know that accuser lied repeatedly under oath in the very courtroom where she now testifies.
You said no.	Id.	Id.
I then asked you what kinds of things you and SSgt Boyfriend would text about, correct?	Id.	Id.

	Accuser's Motions Testimony from 25 November 19.	
You said, "my dad and his mom," correct?	DC – And those text messages were not romantic in nature according to "undetectable" is that correct? NP – Yes sir DC – They were about your father. Correct? NP – Yes sir	Again, showing the panel that she misled the Court under oath at a prior hearing. Once a liar, always a liar.
I'm going to ask you again, under oath, isn't it a fact that you sent SSgt Boyfriend text messages of a sexual nature in the spring of 2018? Isn't it a fact that you sent SSgt Boyfriend a text message that stated I want you? I want to please you? I cannot wait to be with you?	Id.	Id.

117

Question	Cite	Relevance
So, you lied under oath in a hearing before this military judge?	Id.	Id.

Chapter II
My Husband Knows About SSgt Boyfriend, and He's Pissed!

Question	Cite	Relevance
Sometime in the Spring of 2018, your husband finds out that you and SSgt Boyfriend were texting each other? He found out that you two had exchanged dozens and dozens of text messages? He found out that you two were talking nearly every day? He found out that on some days, SSgt Boyfriend called you 4 or 5 times a day?	Husband's Motions Testimony from 25 November 19.	Establishing foundation for accuser's motive to lie. If husband beat up SSgt Boyfriend over text messages and threatened to end their marriage, what would he do if he found out that the accuser had sex with my client?

Your husband got very angry when he found out that you were texting SSgt Boyfriend so much? He got angry when you found out that SSgt Boyfriend called you several times a night?	Accuser's Motions Testimony from 25 November 19. Motions Hearing. "I really don't remember what the text messages said, but I do know that he was angry that it was just a text from him? Q: "The text messages made your husband angry?" A: Yes sir.	Id. Establishing why the accuser is falsely accusing my client.

He got so angry that he called SSgt Boyfriend and confronted him about his relationship with you?		
He got so angry with SSgt Boyfriend that he told SSgt Boyfriend not to call you anymore?		
He got so angry with SSgt Boyfriend that he told SSgt Boyfriend to meet him in the parking lot at the Big Foot mall, right?	Husband's Motions Testimony from 25 November 19.	Id.
Your husband wanted to confront SSgt Boyfriend face to face?		
Your husband got into the car to confront SSgt Boyfriend?		
You got into the car with him?		
In the car, you begged him not to hurt SSgt Boyfriend?		

You told him that the text messages you sent SSgt Boyfriend were only about the gym?

You told your husband the text messages were only about your mother and SSgt Boyfriend's father?

When you arrived at the parking lot, SSgt Boyfriend was already there? You told your husband to not hurt SSgt Boyfriend? Your husband got out of the car and got into SSgt	Accuser's Motions Testimony from 25 November 19. DC – Accuser, where did the confrontation between SSgt. Boyfriend and your husband take place? NP – Umm, I believe it was near the Target down Berkley.	Again, establishing facts to support that the accuser really, really did not want to admit to her husband that she slept with my client. Not only did her husband threaten to end the marriage, but he was also a jealous man with an explosive temper.

Boyfriend's face, right? He wanted to hurt SSgt. Boyfriend?		
Your husband was so angry about these text messages that he threatened to "knock SSgt Boyfriend's teeth down his throat," right?	Husband's Motions Testimony from 25 November 19.	Id.
Your husband grabbed SSgt Boyfriend, right?	Accuser's Motions Testimony from 25 November 19. DC – And you were present for this confrontation? NP – Yes sir.	Id.
You saw them shove each other?	Accuser's Motions Testimony from 25 November 19. "I saw pushing and shoving."	Id.
You saw them punch each other?	Id.	Id.

You even saw your husband and SSgt Boyfriend throw elbows at each other?	Accuser's Motions Testimony from 25 November 19. "Uh…there may have been elbow to faces."	Id.
You were the person who broke up the fight?	Accuser's Motions Testimony from 25 November 19. "They were going back and forth, SSgt Boyfriend had said something but I don't know who swung first but I remember breaking up a fight?"	Id.
The fight lasted three minutes, right?		
Again, that fight was over text messages?	Accuser's Motions Testimony from 25 November 19. DC: How long did the fight last? NP: I'd say three minutes tops.	Id.
SSgt Boyfriend had a black eye?		
SSgt Boyfriend was bleeding from his nose?		
This fight was over text message?		

Chapter III
I MUST Earn Back His Trust

Question	Source	Relevance
Your husband did not leave you after this fight?	Accuser's Motions Testimony from 25 November 19.	Now I need to establish that husband gave accuser a second chance. This means that if the accuser's husband believed that accuser cheated on him again, it would be the end of the marriage.
He did not file for divorce?	Id.	Id.
Despite having difficulties over these text messages, you and your husband decided to work things out?	Accuser's Motions Testimony from 25 November 19. GC – Ok. After this altercation between your husband. SrA Sucker, and SSgt Boyfriend can you just describe your relationship with your husband? NP – Um we got much closer, um that fight kind of like put it into light that I just need to be more careful, and our relationship just got	Id. Again, husband gives her a second chance. Husband will be furious if he finds out that after all this work to rebuild the marriage, the accuser cheated on him again.

Court Martial Cases

	better from that point. Um, we didn't really talk about it for a long time but when we did talk about it, it did resolve a lot of issues and we are still going strong today.	
Your relationship with your husband got better after the fight with SSgt Boyfriend?	Id.	Id.
You worked hard to earn his trust?	Id.	Id.
He worked hard to earn your trust?	Id.	Id.
You wanted your marriage to work?	Id.	Id.
You did not want your husband to leave you?	Id.	Id.
Your marriage is one of the most important things in your life?	Id.	Id.
You have now been married to your husband for over four years.	Id.	Id.
The two of you live together in Japan.	Id.	Id.
The two of you are stationed together in Japan?	Id.	Id.
He traveled with you to this hearing?	Id.	Id.

Chapter V

I was worried that my husband would hear that rumor! Our marriage was just getting strong again, I did not want to explain things to him! He would not have believed me.

Question	Cite	Relevance
Now, I want to talk about why you reported this attempted, alleged sexual assault on 2 November 2018. On 1 November 2018, SrA Batman told you that SSgt Accused was telling people in security forces that you and he had sex during the TDY trip, right? You were angry at SSgt Accused for spreading this rumor about you two, right? It upset you that he told people that you and he were involved in a sexual relationship?	Accuser's Motions Testimony from 25 November 19. DC (1:17:52) – On 1 or 2 November 2017 you heard a rumor from SrA Batman that SSgt Accused was telling people that you and he had hooked up while you were on the TDY. Is that accurate ma'am? NP – No sir, the rumor was that we were engaged in an ongoing relationship and that we were having sex multiple times.	I am establishing that the accuser did not report the alleged sexual assault until she heard a rumor that the accused was telling people they hooked up on TDY. This was very important to the accuser because her husband was stationed on the same base and she did not want these rumors getting back to her husband. She heard the rumors on 2 November 2018 and reported the alleged sexual assault on 3 November 2018, five months after the assault allegedly happened.

You reported this alleged attempted sexual assault to SSgt Police Officer on 2 November 2018, right? In other words, you report this alleged attempted sexual assault within 24 hours of hearing these rumors?	Accuser's Motions Testimony from 25 November 19. DC (1:19:07) – And you first reported this to SSgt Police Officer when I say this you reported the attempted sexual assault to SSgt Police on 2 November 2018 right? NP – Yes sir DC – The day after you heard that rumor? NP – Yes sir	Id.
At this time, you were in the same squadron as SSgt Accused, right?	Accuser's Motions Testimony from 25 November 19.	Id.

As a law enforcement officer, you knew that it was against the law to engage in sexual activities with someone who is not your husband? So, hypothetically, if you had engaged in sex with SSgt Accused, as a married woman, that's something that could receive non-judicial punishment for? Adultery is a violation of the UCMJ? Your unit could even initiate separation against your for engaging in adultery?	Accuser's Motions Testimony from 25 November 19.	Now, I am building upon the idea that the accuser also needed to worry about her career and reputation. If these rumors got back to her command, an investigation may have been initiated. The accuser did not want that.
To make matters worse for you, your husband was still stationed at Big Foot AFB at the time?	Accuser's Motions Testimony from 25 November 19. DC – And at the time your husband was also stationed at Seymour Johnson Air Force Base is that correct? NP – Yes sir	Again, establishing that the accuser's husband worked on the same base and may have heard the rumors as well.

Your husband threatened to knock out SSgt Boyfriend's teeth when your husband found out that you were texting SSgt Boyfriend, right?	Id.	Motive to fabricate. Reminding the jury what the husband did the last time he found out that the accuser was less than faithful. Building upon the accuser's motive to falsely accuse my client.
Your husband got into a fist fight with SSgt Boyfriend over nothing more than text messages, right?	Id.	
So, if your husband found out that you had engaged in sex with SSgt Accused, he most certainly would have gotten extremely angry?	Pretrial interview with accuser.	I typically would not ask this question. However, she had told me this during a pretrial answer and I knew what she was going to say.
If your husband heard that you and SSgt Accused had sex, it may have destroyed all that trust you had been building with him since the SSgt Boyfriend text messages?	Id.	Id.

The Takeaway

The cross-examination of the prosecution's witness tells your story by exposing false claims and revealing the truth. Effective cross-examination requires that your attorney:

- Know in advance what the witness is going to say, and prepare the line of questioning accordingly.
- Ask brief questions that focused only on eliciting the answers that will directly help your case.
- Listen carefully to the witness' answers and be ready to adjust the line of questioning on the fly.
- Ask the most powerful questions at the start and the conclusion of the examination.

Closing Argument

Chapter 14

The closing argument is your attorney's final word in your trial. It needs to be strong, credible, and convincing. It should reiterate the theory and themes of the case and connect the facts brought out during the trial to those claims. Any weaknesses in your case should be addressed here, and the panel reminded that the burden of proof is on the side of the prosecution. Rhetorical questions at this stage can be very effective. The closing argument should conclude with an appeal to the panel to find in your favor.

The culmination of the fight has arrived. Maximus is staring down Commodus, and the final conflict is at hand. The courtroom is packed, the judge asks if your attorney is prepared to present closing argument, and your attorney takes center stage. Few things in life rouse my blood like standing in front of a packed courtroom ready to argue as forcefully as I can against injustice, hypocrisy, and lies. The rubber has now met the road, and the only thing left that matters is whether your attorney has the skill, power, and confidence to deliver under pressure.

Closing Argument Organization. The drama in the courtroom is at an all-time high when your attorney starts her argument. However, this is when the fundamentals matter the most. A strong closing argument is an organized closing argument. I take extra measures to ensure that my arguments flow logically and directly mirror the themes and theories from my opening statement. In the first minute of my closing argument, I take the panel right back to my theory of the case. I hit those three or four themes that we talked about in the opening statement, those same themes that I developed during cross-examination.

I think of a trial like one interwoven narrative. Nothing is done in isolation. Everything is done with purpose and force. In opening, I introduce my theme and theories; in cross, I develop those themes; and during our case-in-chief, I highlight those themes. Now, in closing, I hammer those themes home. Much like a great novel, movie, or play, everything connects with everything else. A great closing statement should put everything together for the panel; it should answer their questions, and it should be easy for them to follow.

The first minute or two of the closing argument are the most important of the entire argument. I like to start my closing argument by mirroring my opening statement; this builds credibility and trust with the panel. I like to start with something like the following:

> *Theme:* "Ladies and Gentlemen, I told you during the opening statement that this is a case about an accuser who will do whatever she can to save her marriage, career, and reputation." *Theories:* "Now, let us talk about the facts of this case; the same facts we discussed together in opening:
>
> First. PFC Jane was married when she sent my client nude pictures. She was married when she sent my client a text message at 2300 to come to her house. She was married when she had sex with my client. As she admitted under oath, she did not report this alleged assault until her husband found her

phone. And as you saw firsthand, she is now doing everything she can to save her marriage. PFC Janes has a motive to lie to you.

Second. You found out that minutes before PFC Jane met with CID, she deleted all the text messages she sent to my client. She deleted all the Facebook messages she sent to my client. And she deleted all the pictures that she sent to my client. PFC Jane destroyed evidence in this case. She does not want you to know the truth. She does not want you to know what really happened in this case. You cannot trust PFC Jane. Honest people do not delete evidence. Honest people do not hide evidence. Honest people do not falsely accuse someone of sexual assault. PFC Jane is not an honest person.

Third. During my opening statement, I told you that the government could not produce a single eyewitness to corroborate what PFC Jane said happened. How come the government did not call anyone from the party to testify? How come the government did not call the nurse who performed the SAFE exam? How come the government did not call a single member of law enforcement? The only witnesses that you heard from were called by the defense. We want you to know the truth. The defense has nothing to hide. In fact, our witnesses told you that moments after allegedly being assaulted, PFC Jane played beer pong, danced with our client, and appeared to be having a wonderful time. Does this make sense to you? Has the government explained this to you? Let us be blunt: there is no evidence to support PFC Jane's version of events.

Ladies and gentlemen, as I stated in the opening statement, this is not a case about a young woman being assaulted—this is a case about a young woman doing everything in her power to hide the truth to save her marriage. Now, let us talk about why the government has not proven this case beyond a reasonable doubt.

As you can see, I have taken full advantage of the first two minutes of my closing argument. I hit hard, reiterated my theme and my theories, and went on the attack. More importantly, I maintained my credibility with the jury. I told them in opening statement to trust me, and I delivered. I have put my client in the best possible position, and I have kept my word. You see now why over-promising in opening statements can crush your case. Credibility is king.

Developing Your Theories. Once I have concisely reintroduced my theories to the panel, I further develop each theory of the case with facts brought out during the trial. Again, this maintains my credibility and keeps things simple for the panel. Here is what the argument will sound like.

Theory 1: I now want to load my theory with facts. I do not resuscitate every fact that supported the theory, and I do not repeat every word of the witnesses' testimony. Instead, I hit hard, do not waste time, and I use the most helpful facts to pound home my version of events. Your attorney should not simply restate what the witnesses said. Your attorney needs to argue, fight, and deliver. Below, I use my cross-examination of the accuser and her husband to hammer home the truth—the accuser had a motive to lie. With my first theory of defense, I want the panel to think: "hmm....she is trying to save her marriage. That makes a lot of sense to me. I'm just not sure I can trust her."

> *PFC Jane has a motive to lie in this case. She was desperate to save her marriage. Let us talk in more detail about that now. During cross-examination, PFC Jane admitted that she was married. She admitted that she could get in big trouble for committing adultery while serving the Air Force. She admitted that she sent my client nude photos. She admitted that she had sex with my client and tried to hide it from her husband. And she admitted, under oath, that she only accused my client of sexual assault after her husband discovered the text messages she sent to my client.*
>
> *PFC Jane's husband testified that he was furious when he*

found out about his wife's alleged affair. Immediately after seeing the text messages exchanged between my client and his wife, he told PFC Jane that he wanted a divorce and that their marriage was over. Then, after he made that threat, for the very first time, PFC Jane claims that my client assaulted her. Ladies and gentlemen, PFC Jane has a motive to lie. Her story, her words, and her version of events are tainted and stained by her desire to save her marriage, her desire to avoid taking responsibility for her actions, and now my client stands before you unjustly charged with a heinous crime that he did not commit. Does that sound like justice?

The only way you can convict my client is if the government proves their case beyond a reasonable doubt. This means the government must prove its case to an evidentiary certainty. Ladies and gentlemen, I could stop right now, and this case would be saturated in doubt. PFC Jane has a motive to lie, and she cannot be trusted to tell the truth.

Theory 2: I now want to load my second theory with facts. Again, do not bore the panel with a blanket recital of the facts presented in trial. They were there, and they know what was said. Instead, hit hard, focus on the most important points, and take no prisoners. Here, I want the panel to think to themselves: "how can we trust someone who deletes evidence? What is she trying to hide?"

Ladies and gentlemen, PFC Jane cannot be trusted. She deleted evidence. She destroyed evidence. Let us talk about what we know. PFC Jane admitted during cross-examination that right before she met with CID, she deleted over 75 messages and pictures that she sent to my client. She claimed that she was simply embarrassed to show CID the sexual messages. That may be true, but she also did not want CID to see the truth. She did not want them to see that she consented to having sex with my client; she did not want CID to know that she sent my client nude pictures of herself days after

> *allegedly being assaulted, and she did not want her husband to find out the whole truth. She deleted those messages to save her marriage. She deleted those messages, and, as a result, she robbed you, the panel, of deciding for yourselves what really happened here.*
>
> *She obstructed this investigation. If my client had destroyed evidence, he would have been charged; he would have been condemned, and the prosecutor would be arguing for you to make him pay. But PFC Jane admitted on the stand that she is not facing any repercussions for obstructing this investigation. Does that sound fair to you? Does that sound just to you? Here is the truth: you cannot trust a person who deletes evidence; you cannot trust a person who destroys evidence, and you cannot trust PFC Jane. She has proven time and again that she is willing to do whatever it takes to save her marriage, her reputation, and her career. How can you trust a person who is willing to break the law to save herself? Again, I say, the government has failed to satisfy their burden. This case, as I stand here now, I saturated in doubt.*

Theory 3: Here, I want the jury to ask themselves whether PFC Jane's story makes sense. I want them to wonder why nobody else suspected anything, saw anything, or heard anything. I also want them to consider whether it is just to convict someone in a "he said, she said" case when the accuser's story simply does not add up.

> *Ladies and gentlemen, PFC Jane claims that she screamed, that she fought off my client, and that my client grabbed her neck and face with force. Well…where are the witnesses? She was around an entire platoon's worth of airmen just a few hours after the alleged assault. Not one person saw a scratch on her face. Not one person saw a red mark on her neck. In fact, what did we find out? We learned that after the alleged assault, she went back to the party. She drank more. She socialized more. And, by all accounts, she had a good time at the party.*

> *Does this make sense? Does this sound like a person who was sexually assaulted minutes before?*
>
> *Again, the government has the burden. They must prove this case to an evidentiary certainty. Well…where are the witnesses? Where is the physical evidence? How come the government cannot produce even one person to say that PFC Jane appeared to be having a hard time at the party? Where is the evidence? Here is the sad truth: my client is facing a sex assault trial based on nothing more than the word of a single witness who has a motive to fabricate and who destroys evidence to hide the truth. This is not proof beyond a reasonable doubt. This is a case saturated in doubt.*

Address Weaknesses. Much of your attorney's closing argument needs to focus on the strengths of your case and the weaknesses in the government's case. Every trial will have some weaknesses. If it did not, the case would likely not have been prosecuted. At this point in the trial, I like to address the major weaknesses I see. I do not spend as much time here, but I do address it. I do this because I hope to take the wind out of the government's sails, and I believe it builds credibility with the panel. I recently had a trial where the accuser sent my client several messages over text accusing him of raping her. My client responded with several texts that read like this:

> "OMG….I'm so sorry. I would never have done that if I was sober."
>
> "Please don't tell people that I raped you. It could ruin my career."
>
> "I never meant to hurt you. I was just so drunk. I promise that I'll never drink like that again."

On the surface, these messages are not good. In opening, the prosecutor focused much of their case on these text messages and argued that my client admitted to assaulting the accuser. This is how I addressed these text messages:

> *In opening statement, the government argued that my client admitted to sexually assaulting his accuser. In fact, they have based their entire case on a few messages sent from my client to the complaining witness the morning after the alleged assault. Let us talk about these messages together, as honestly as possible. My client is a 22-year-old airman. He has been told in briefings, incorrectly, time and again, that it is sexual assault to "hook up" with a fellow airman who is drinking. He knew that his accuser loved attention. He knew that his accuser loves drama. And he knew that regardless of what he said, his accuser was going to tell all her friends and coworkers that my client sexually assaulted her. He did not want to be accused. He was terrified. He was afraid. You must ask yourselves, in light of all of the evidence that you have now seen, are those the text messages of a guilty man, or are those the text messages of a scared young person who does not know what to say?*

Argue Burden of Proof and Ask Rhetorical Questions. Once I address perceived weaknesses in my case, I strive to finish on a strong note. The burden of proof in a criminal case always falls on the government, and that burden is a high bar to meet. I want to force the government to argue the weaknesses in their case during their rebuttal argument. I do this by hammering home the burden of proof issue and asking rhetorical questions that I know they cannot answer. Often, I will do this by again relying on my theories of the case. It will look something like this:

> *I want to remind you again that the burden of proof is on the government. It is their job to prove this case to you beyond a reasonable doubt, the highest burden of proof in American law. The military judge defined what beyond a reasonable doubt is, and I want to discuss that for a moment. Beyond a reasonable doubt means that the government must prove this case to an evidentiary certainty. Let me repeat that: The government must prove this case to an evidentiary certainty.*

The defense does not have a burden to prove in this case. The defense does not need to call a single witness. As my client sits here today, he is cloaked in the presumption of innocence. That presumption can only be lifted if the government has answered for you all the questions they need to answer to prove this case to an evidentiary certainty.

I ask you, has the government done this? Have they extinguished all reasonable doubt in your minds? Have they proven this case to an evidentiary certainty? Did they explain to you why the accuser only reported this case after her husband accused her of cheating? Did they explain to you why the accuser deleted evidence and misled law enforcement? Did they properly explain to you why the accuser went back to the party and continued to drink after the alleged assault? The accuser herself says that she had to fight my client off her. Well, how come not a single witness observed so much as a scratch on her face? The accuser claimed that she yelled at my client to stop, but nobody in the hotel next door heard anything. Does that make sense?

Ladies and gentlemen of the panel, these unanswered questions are reasonable doubt. In short, the government cannot satisfy their burden in the case. Even after three days of trial and an investigation that lasted more than a year, we have unanswered questions. I submit to you, again, this case is saturated in doubt, and the government has fallen well short of its burden.

Conclusion. Once I thoroughly articulate that the government has failed to satisfy their burden, I move to conclude my argument. In my conclusion, I do not get fancy and say things like, "As such, I request that you fully acquit my client of each charge and specification." No. I like to speak to the panel as I speak to my friends, telling them exactly what I want. I also rehash one last time the theories of my case.

I have now reached the most difficult part of the trial for a

> *defense attorney...the end. I have nothing more to argue, which terrifies me. I hope that you now see that my client is not guilty of this crime and that he has been falsely accused by a person who would do anything to save her marriage, career, and reputation. She lied to her husband, she deleted evidence, and she has a motive to lie. Considering those facts, ladies, and gentlemen, I simply ask that you let my client go home. That you find my client not guilty, and you put an end to this nightmare. I ask, humbly, that you find my client not guilty and let him walk out of here a free man. Thank you.*

A good attorney understands that closing argument is the most dramatic part of the trial. However, a good closing argument is built piece-by-piece throughout the course of the trial. The closing must be interwoven into one single narrative throughout the duration of the trial. Your attorney should restate their themes and theories; fill in those themes with facts developed during trial; address weaknesses; hammer home the burden by asking rhetorical questions, and candidly tell the panel to let you go. If your attorney can do these things, he has put you in a position to succeed. Like most things in trial, this comes with careful attention to detail, skill, storytelling ability, rigorous preparation, and some luck.

The Takeaway

The closing argument brings everything together, and shows how all of the facts in the case lead inevitability to one conclusion: you are not guilty of the crime of which you stand accused. A successful closing argument will:

- Remind the panel of the theory and themes of your case.
- Show that the facts in the case support the themes and theories.
- Address any weaknesses in your case.

- Remind the panel that the burden of proof in a criminal trial is on the prosecution. Rhetorical questions can be very effective here.
- Forthrightly ask the panel to accept the argument and release you from the charge.

Conclusion

Court Martial Cases: Defense Strategies and Best Practices offers an informative tour through the legal process that begins with the accusation of a criminal offense and culminates in a court-martial. Throughout this tour, one thing above all becomes clear: a skilled defense team can make all the difference. Robert F. Capovilla and Mickey Williams' guide teaches you what you need to know to make smart decisions and participate as an informed member of that team. Chapter by chapter, Capovilla and Williams lay out the legal process that brings an accused service member to court-martial, highlighting the best strategies for a strong case and a fair and just result.

Breaking down the court-martial process into two parts—the period leading up to the trial, where evidence is gathered and the formal aspects of the trial established, and the trial itself—the guide tells you what you need to know, when you need to know it. For the pre-trial period, the guide emphasizes the importance of evidence-gathering and legal savvy in laying the groundwork for the trial. Some key takeaways:

Conclusion

- Charges against you are preferred based on the findings of law enforcement and the prosecutor during their initial investigations. You need an attorney at this stage to conduct a separate investigation on your behalf. Presented during the Article 32 hearing, the findings of your attorney's investigation can significantly impact the way the charges are framed.
- At your arraignment hearing, you'll be asked to plead guilty or not guilty to the preferred charges. If your attorney believes there might be more information pertinent to your case that he isn't yet in possession of, he may advise you to defer pleading either way.
- The discovery phase commences after the arraignment hearing. Each side is obligated by the rules of discovery to share with the other all the evidence in their possession, including witness testimony. Having this information in hand allows your attorney to begin building your case.

All of the careful preparation of the pre-trial period pays off during the trial itself. With a firm grasp on all of the facts of the case, your attorney will come to trial armed with an accurate theory of defense and the themes to support it. With a solid defense team, you can expect consistency, clarity, and a compelling narrative to predominate throughout the trial. Here's what to look for:

- Not only will your attorney rigorously question every potential panelist to select service men and women who are open-minded and fair, he will use the voir dire process to win their confidence and trust.
- Your attorney's opening statement at the trial will clearly establish your side's theory of the case and its themes. It will tell your story of the events in

- question in such a way that the panelists relive those events from your perspective.
- Your attorney's questions for the witnesses called for direct examination will open the way for your story to be told again, from the witnesses' perspective and in their own words. When your attorney interrogates the government's witnesses in cross-examination, carefully prepared questions will expose the contradictions and errors in your accuser's story and reinforce your own.
- All of the threads in the case, including evidence and the revelations brought out in witness testimony, are brought together in your attorney's closing argument. A skilled attorney will use these threads to again tell your story. He will reiterate his theory of the case and its themes, and ask the panel to find in your favor.

For legal representation and counsel, you might choose to wait for a military defense attorney to be detailed to your case after your Article 32 hearing. You are also entitled to bring on outside counsel of your own choosing. You may do this at any time during this process, although from what you've learned here about this process you know that the earlier you make this call, the better. If you do choose to hire a civilian attorney to represent you, your detailed attorney will remain on your team.

Robert F. Capovilla and Mickey Williams invite you to contact their firm, Capovilla & Williams, for a free consultation. They've already helped thousands of other service members, and bring expertise and experience to every case. Call 855-442-6271 or visit military-defenseattorney.com to find out how they can help you.

www.ingramcontent.com/pod-product-compliance
Lightning Source LLC
Chambersburg PA
CBHW071712020426
42333CB00017B/2232